# THOMAS TROWARD'S
Bible Mystery and Bible Meaning
"without the jargon"

----------

Written
through the character of
Richard Dale Lode

----------

*TRUTH CENTER Publishing*

----------

Conversion
(07-12-14)

*Copyrigh*t© 2013

### You can purchase Mr. Lode's books at:

*Barnes and Noble - - - BN.com*

*Amazon.com*

**truthcenter.blog.com**
*his website*

**Books are also available on Kindle**

------------------

**"Experiencing" THE HIDDEN MAGIC** *"at the Center"*

**NEW AGE BIBLE**
*"New Thought for the $3^{rd}$ Millennium"*

**A SHORT COURSE in Miracles**
*"The Holy Bible's $3^{rd}$ Testament"*

**Finding the Essential "CHRIST"**
***"The Bible's last Testament"***

**A SEARCH FOR "SELF"**
*"Experiencing A Course in Miracles"*

**WINNING** *"at the Game of Life"*

**THE HIDDEN MAGIC** *"at the Center"*

**The GOSPEL of THOMAS** *"In Modern Day Language"*

**The Essential THOMAS TROWARD**

**THOMAS TROWARD'S**
Bible Mystery and Bible Meaning
"without the jargon"

--------

## FOREWORD

If this book helps the reader to see the intelligible sequence between cause and effect in God's creation of man its purpose has been fulfilled.

*"Bible Mystery and Bible Meaning - without the jargon"* is an accurate teaching of the Bible and will one day be seen as part of a great spiritual awakening.

**Review of Books**
*TRUTH CENTER Publishing*

----------

## THOMAS TROWARD'S
Bible Mystery and Bible Meaning
"without the jargon"

## Chapter 1
## THE CREATION

The Bible, rightly interpreted, is the Book of Man's deliverance from sorrow and sickness, from poverty, struggle, and uncertainty, from ignorance and limitations, and finally from death itself.

This may appear to be "a tall order," but nevertheless this is exactly what it promises, and it professes to contain the secret whereby this happy condition of perfect liberty may be attained.

Jesus says that if a man keeps his saying he shall never see death: in the Book of Job we are told that if a man has with him "a messenger, an interpreter," he shall be delivered from death, *and shall return to the days of his youth*: the Psalms speak of our renewing our youth: and yet again we are told that by acquainting ourselves with God we shall be at peace, we shall layup gold as dust and have plenty of silver, we shall decree a thing and it shall be established unto us.

Now, what I propose is that we shall re-read the Bible with the idea that Jesus and these other speakers really meant what they said. Of course, from the standpoint of the traditional interpretation this is a startling proposition.

The first thing to notice is that there is a common element running through the texts I have quoted; they all contain the idea of acquiring certain information, and the promised results are all based on our getting this information, and using it.

Jesus says it depends on our keeping his saying, that is, receiving the information which he had to give and acting upon it.

Job says that it depends on rightly interpreting a certain message, and again that it depends on our making ourselves acquainted with something; and the context of the passage in *the Psalms makes it clear that the deliverance from death and the renewal of youth "there promised"* are to be attained through the "ways" which the Lord "made known."

In all these passages we find that these wonderful results come from the attainment of certain knowledge, and the Bible therefore appeals to our Reason. From this point of view we may speak of the Science of the Bible, and as we advance in our study, we shall find that this is not a misuse of terms, for the Bible is scientific; only its science is not primarily physical but mental.

The Bible speaks of Man as being composed of "Spirit, soul, and body" (1 Thess. 5:23), or in other words as combining into a single unity a threefold nature --- spiritual, psychic, and physical; and the knowledge which it proposes to give us is the knowledge of the true relation between these three factors. The Bible also speaks of the totality of all Being, manifested and un-manifested, as likewise constituting a threefold unity, which may be termed, "God", "Man", and "the Universe"; and it occupies itself with telling us of the interaction, both positive and negative, which goes on between these three. Furthermore, it bases this interaction upon two great psychological laws, namely, that of the creative power of Thought and that of the amenability of Thought to control by Suggestion; and it affirms that this Creative Power is as innately inherent in Man's Thought as in the Divine Thought.

But it also shows how through ignorance of these truths we unknowingly misuse our creative power, and so produce the evils we deplore.

Seen in this light, the Bible is found **not** to be a mere collection of old-world fables or unintelligible dogmas, but a statement of great universal law and this universal law is in the realm of the invisible as well as in the realm of the visible, and therefore it deals with the facts of the spiritual nature as well as with those on the physical plane; and accordingly it takes into consideration an earlier process which takes place before Evolution --- the process, namely, of Involution, the act of looking within before looking without.

But Involution and Evolution are not opposed to one another; they are only the earlier and later stages of the same process: the perpetual urging onward of Spirit for Self-expression in infinite varieties. And therefore the grand foundation on which the whole Bible system is built up is that the Spirit, which is thus continually passing into manifestation, is always the *same* Spirit. In other words, it is only ONE.

These two fundamental truths, Involution and Evolution --- are the basis of all that the Bible has to teach us, and therefore from its first page to its last, we shall find these two ideas continually recurring in a variety of different connections: the ONE-ness of the Divine Spirit and the Creative Power of man's Thought, which the Bible expresses in its two grand statements, that "God is ONE", and that Man is made "in the image and likeness of God".

These are the two fundamental statements of the Bible, and all its other statements flow logically from them. And since the whole argument of Scripture is built up from these premises, the reader must not be surprised at the frequency with which our analysis of that argument will bring us back to these two initial propositions. So far from being a vain repetition, this continual reduction of the statements of the Bible to the premises with which it originally sets out is the strongest proof that we have in them a sure and solid foundation on which to base our present life and our future expectations.

## "In the Beginning"

The opening announcement that "in the beginning God created the heaven and the earth" contains the statement of the first of two propositions which are the fundamental premises from which the whole Bible is evolved. From the Master's instruction to the woman of Samaria we know that "God" means "Spirit" --- that is, Spirit in the Universal. Thus the opening words of the Bible may be read, "in the beginning Spirit" - the underlying Universal Unity created the heaven and the earth.

This statement --- that God created the heaven and the earth --- brings us to the consideration of the Bible way of using words. The fact that the Bible deals with spiritual and psychic matters makes it of necessity an esoteric book, and therefore, in common with all other esoteric literature, it makes a symbolic use of words for the purpose of succinctly expressing ideas which would otherwise require elaborate explanation, and also for the purpose of concealing its meaning from those who are not yet safely to be entrusted with it. But this need not discourage the earnest student, for by comparing one part of the Bible with another he will find that the Bible itself affords the clue to the translation of its own symbolical vocabulary.

Here, as in so many other instances, the Master has given us the key to the right interpretation. He says that the Kingdom of Heaven is *within* us; in other words, that "Heaven" is the kingdom of the innermost and spiritual; and if so, then by necessary implication "Earth" must be the symbol of the opposite extreme and must metaphorically mean the outermost and material. We are starting the history of the evolution of the world in which we live; that is to say, this Power, which the Bible calls "God," is first presented to us in the opening words of Genesis at a stage immediately preceding the beginning of a stupendous work.

Now what are the conditions necessary for the doing of any work? Obviously there must be something that works and something that is worked upon --- an active and a passive factor; an energy and a material on or in which that energy operates. This, then, is what is meant by the creation of Heaven and Earth; it is that operation of the eternally subsisting ONE upon Itself which produces its dual expression as Individual Energy and Psychic Substance. But this does not mean a *separation*, for Energy can only be exhibited by reason of something which is energized; or, in other words, for Life to manifest at all, there must be something that lives. This is an all-important truth, for *our conception of ourselves as beings separate from the Divine Life is the root of all our troubles.*

In its first verse, therefore, the Bible starts us with the conception of Energy or *Life inherent in substance* and shows us that the two constitute a dual-unity which is the first manifestation of the Infinite, the Un-manifested ONE; and if the reader will think these things out for himself, he will see that these are primary intuitions the contrary of which it is impossible to conceive.

But *we are* particularly *cautioned against the mistake of supposing that Substance is the same thing as Form*, for we are told that the "earth was without form." No! that primordial state of Substance with which the opening verse of the Bible is concerned is something very far removed from any conception we can have of Matter as formed into atoms or electrons. We are here only at the first stage of Involution, and the presence of material atoms is a stage, and by no means the earliest, in the process of Evolution.

We are next told that the Spirit of God moved upon the face of the waters. Here we have two factors, "Spirit" and "Water", and the initial movement is attributed to Spirit. This verse introduces us to that particular mode of manifestation of the Universal Substance which we may call the Psychic. This Psychic mode of the Universal Substance may best be described as Cosmic Soul, Psychic not yet differentiated into any individual forms. This is "the Soul of the Universe." It is the universal psychic medium in which forms take their inception in obedience to the movement of Spirit, or Thought. This is the realm of *Potential* Forms, and is the connecting link between Spirit and Matter, and as such plays a most important part in the composition of the Cosmos and of Man.

The existence of this intermediary between Spirit and Matter must never be lost sight of. We may call it the Distributive Medium. In passing through it the hitherto undistributed Energy of Spirit receives differentiation of direction and so ultimately produces differentiation of forms and relationships on the outermost or visible plane. This is the Cosmic Psychic Element which is esoterically called "Water", and we have the utterance of a high authority on this subject, for the Master himself concentrates his whole instruction to Nicodemus on the point that the New Birth results from the interaction of "Spirit" and "Water," especially emphasizing the fact that "the flesh" has no share in the operation. This distinction between "the flesh", or the outermost principle, and "Water" should be carefully noted. The emphasis laid by the Master on the nothingness of "the flesh" and the essentialness of "Water" must mark a distinction of the most important kind, and we shall find it very helpful in unraveling the meaning of many passages of the Bible to grasp this distinction at the outset. The action of "Spirit" upon "Water" is that of an active upon a passive principle; and the result of any sort of Work is to reconstruct the material worked upon into a form which it did not possess before. Now the new form to be produced, whatever it may be, is a *result* and therefore is not to be counted among the causes of its own production.

Hence it is a self-obvious truism that any act of creative power must take place at a more interior level than that of the form to be created, and accordingly, whether in the Old or the New Testament, the creative action is always contemplated as taking place between the Spirit and the Water. Whether we are thinking of producing a new world or a new man, we must always go back to this First Cause.

We are told that the first product of the movement of Spirit upon Water or the Psychic was Light, but the statement that the Sun was not created till the fourth day guards us against the mistake of supposing that what is here meant is the light visible to the physical eye. Rather, it is that All-pervading Inner Psychic Light, of which I shall have more to say by and by, and which only becomes visible as the corresponding sense of inward vision begins to be developed.

The initial Light having thus been produced, we see the introduction of the firmament on the second and on the third day the emanation of Earth from "the Water," or the production of the actual physical system of Nature --- the commencement of the process of Evolution. Up to this point the action has been entirely upon the inner plane of "Water" --- that is to say, a process of Involution --- and consistently with this it was impossible for the heavenly bodies to begin giving physical light until the fourth day, for until then no physical sun or planets could have existed.

With the fourth day, however, the physical universe is differentiated into shape; and on the fifth day the *terrestrial* waters begin to take their share in the evolutionary process by spontaneously producing fish. The terrestrial earth, already on the third day impregnated with the vegetable principle, takes up the evolutionary work on the sixth day, producing all those other animal races which had not already originated in the waters, and the preparation of the world as an abode for Man is completed.

It would be difficult to give a more concise statement of Evolution. Originating Spirit subsists at first as simple Unity; then it differentiates itself into the active and passive principles spoken of as "Heaven" and "Earth," or "Spirit" and "Water." From these proceed Light, *then the work done on the interior planes is reproduced in physical manifestation*, thus marking a still further unfoldment; and finally, in the phrases "let the waters bring forth" and "let the earth bring forth," the land and water of our habitable globe are distinctly stated to be the sources from which all vegetable and animal forms have been evolved. Thus creation is described as the self-transforming action of the ONE un-analyzable Spirit passing by successive transitions into all the varieties of manifestations that fill the Universe.

And here we may notice a point which has puzzled commentators unacquainted with the principles on which the Bible is written. This is the expression "the evening and the morning were the first day and the evening and the morning were the second day and the evening and the morning were the third day, etc". Why, it is asked, does each day begin with the evening? Because the second verse of the Bible tells us that the starting-point was Darkness, and the coming forth of Light out of Darkness cannot be stated in any other order than the dawning of morning from night. It is the dawning into manifestation out of non-manifestation, and this happens at each successive stage of the evolutionary process. We should notice, also, that nothing is said as to the remainder of each day. All that we hear of each day is "the morning," thus indicating the grand truth that when once a Divine day opens, it never again descends into the shades of night. It is always "morning." What a glorious and inspiring truth: when once God begins a work, that work will never cease, but will go on forever expanding into more and more radiant forms of strength and beauty, because it is the expression of the Infinite, which is Itself Love, Wisdom, and Power.

Man is no exception to the Universal Law of Evolution. It has often been remarked that the account of his creation is twofold. First we are told of the creation in the realm of the invisible and psychic --- that is to say, the process of Involution; and afterwards we are told of the creation on the plane of the concrete and material --- that is to say, the process of Evolution. And since Involution is the cause and Evolution the effect, the Bible observes this order both in the account of the creation of the world and in that of the creation of Man. In regard to his physical structure, Man's body, we are told, is formed from the "earth" --- that is, by a combination of the same material elements as all other concrete forms; and thus in the physical Man, the evolutionary process attains its culmination in the production of a material vehicle capable of serving as the starting-point for a further advance, which has now to be made on the Intellectual and Spiritual.

The principle of Evolution is never departed from, but its further action now includes the intelligent co-operation of the evolving Individuality itself as a necessary factor in the work. The development of merely animal Man is the spontaneous operation of Nature, *but the development of the mental Man can only result from his own recognition of the Law of Self-expression of Spirit as operating in himself.*

It is, therefore, for the setting forth of Man's power to use this Law that this interpretation of the Bible was written; and accordingly, the great fact on which it seeks to rivet our attention in its first utterance regarding Man is that he is made in the image and likeness of God. A very little reflection will show us that this likeness cannot be in the outward form, for the Universal Spirit in which all things subsist cannot be limited by shape. It is a Principle permeating all things as their innermost substance and life-giving energy, and of it the Bible tells us that "in the beginning" there was nothing else.

Now the one and only conception we can have of this Universal Life-Principle is that of the Creative Power producing infinitely varied expressions of itself by Thought, for we cannot ascribe any other initial mode of movement to Spirit but that of thought. *The likeness, therefore, between God and man must be a mental likeness*, and since the only fact which, up to this point, the Bible has told us regarding the Universal Mind is its Creative Power, the resemblance indicated can only consist in the reproduction of the same Creative Power in the Mind of Man.

As we progress, we shall find that the whole Bible turns on this one fundamental fact. The Creative Power is inherent in our Thought, and we can by no means divest ourselves of it; but because we are ignorant that we possess this power, or because we misapprehend the conditions for its beneficial employment, we need much instruction in the nature of our own as yet unrecognized possibilities; and it is the purpose of the Bible to give us this teaching.

A little consideration of the terms of the evolutionary process will show us that since there is no other source from which it can proceed, the Individual Mind, which is *the essential entity that we call Man, can be no other than a concentration of the Universal Mind into individual consciousness*. Man's Mind is, therefore, a miniature reproduction of the Divine Mind with all its Divine qualities, just as fire has always the same igneous qualities whether the center of combustion be large or small; and so it is upon this fact that the Bible fixes our attention from first to last. And further, if the human mind is the exact image and likeness of the Divine, then its creative power must be equally unlimited. Its *mode* is different, being directed to the individual and particular, but its *quality* is the same; and this becomes evident if we reflect that it is not possible to set any limit to Thought, and that its only limitations are such as are set by the limited conceptions of the individual who thinks. And it is precisely here that the difficulty comes in. Our Thought must necessarily be limited by our conceptions. We cannot think of something which we cannot conceive; and therefore, the more limited our conceptions, the more limited will be our thought, and its creations will accordingly be limited in a corresponding degree.

## Chapter 2
## THE FALL

### Eden

In the last chapter we reached the conclusion that in the nature of things, Thought must always be limited by the range of the intelligence which gives rise to it. The power of Thought as the creative agent is perfectly unlimited in itself, but its action is limited by the particular conception which it is sent forth to embody. If it is a wide conception based upon an enlarged perception of truth, the thought which dwells upon it will produce corresponding conditions. This is self-evident; it is simply the statement that an instrument will not do work to which the hand of the workman does not apply it; and if the student will only fix this very simple idea in his mind, he will find in it the key to the whole mystery of man's power of self-evolution. Let us make our first use of this key to unlock the mystery of the story of Eden.

It is hardly necessary to say that the story of Eden is an allegory: that is clearly shown by the nature of the two trees that grew in the center of the garden --- the Tree of the Knowledge of Good and Evil and the Tree of Life. This allegory is one repeated in many lands and ages, and the meaning of the story is always the same. The garden is the Garden of the Soul, and the Tree of Life is that innermost perception of Spirit of which the Master said that it would be a well of water springing up to everlasting life to all who realized it. It is the garden which elsewhere in Scripture is called "the garden of the Lord"; and in accordance with the nature of the garden, the plants which grow in it, and which man has to tend and cultivate, are thoughts and ideas; and the chief of them are his idea of Life and his idea of Knowledge, and these occupy the center of the garden because all our ideas must take their color from them.

We must recollect that human life is a drama whose action takes place in three worlds, and therefore, in interpreting the Bible, we must always make sure which world, at any moment, we are reading about --- the spiritual, the intellectual, or the physical. In the spiritual world, which is that of the supreme ideal, there exists nothing but the potential of the absolutely perfect; and it is on this account that in the opening chapter of the Bible we read that God saw that all his work was good --- the Divine eye could find no flaw anywhere; and we should note carefully that this absolutely good creation included Man also.

But as soon as we descend to the Intellectual world, which is the world of man's *conception* of things, it is quite different; and until man comes to realize the truly spiritual, and therefore perfectly good essential nature of all things, there is room for any amount of *mis*-conception, resulting in a corresponding misdirection of man's creative instrument of Thought, which thus produces correspondingly misinformed realities.

Now the perfect life of Adam and Eve in Eden is the picture of Man as he exists in the spiritual world. It is not the tradition of some bygone age, but a symbolical representation of what we all are in our innermost being. In *the Gospel of Thomas* the Master was ask when the Kingdom of Heaven would come and he replied, "When that which is without shall be as that which is within" --- in other words, when the perfection of the innermost spiritual essence shall be reproduced in the external part. In the allegory, Man is warned by God that Death will be the consequence of eating the fruit of the tree of the Knowledge of Good and Evil. This is not the threat of a sentence to be passed by God, but a warning as to the nature of the fruit itself; but this warning is disregarded by Eve, and she shares the forbidden fruit with Adam, and they are both expelled from Eden and become subject to Death as the consequence.

Now if Eden is the garden of the Soul, it is clear that Adam and Eve cannot be separate persons, but must be two principles in the human individuality which are so closely united as to be represented by a wedded pair. What, then, are these principles? St Paul makes a very remarkable statement regarding Adam and Eve. He tells us that "Adam was not deceived, but the woman being deceived was in the transgression" (1 Tim. 2:14). We have, therefore, Bible warrant for saying that Adam was not deceived; but at the same time, the story of the fall clearly shows that he was expelled from Eden for partaking of the fruit of Eve's instigation.

To satisfy both statements, therefore, we are required to find in Adam and Eve two principles, one of which is capable of being deceived, and is deceived, and falls in consequence of the deception; and the other of which is incapable of being deceived but yet is involved with the fall of the former. This is the problem which has to be worked out, and the names of Adam and Eve supply the solution. Eve, we are told, was so called because she was the mother of all living (Gen. 3:20). Eve, then, is the Mother of Life, a subject to which I shall have to refer to again in a later chapter. Eve, signifies Breath --- the principle which we are told in Genesis 2:7 constitutes Man a living Soul. Adam is rendered as "earth" or as "Not-breath". And thus in these two names we have the description of two principles, one of which is "Breath" and Life-conveying, while the other is "Not-breath" and is nothing but earth. It requires no great skill to recognize in these the Soul and the Body.

Any work on physiology will tell you that the human body is made up of certain chemical materials --- so much chalk, so much carbon, so much water, etc. Obviously these substances cannot be deceived because they have no intelligence, and any deception that occurs must be accepted by the soul or intellectual principle, which is Eve, the mother of the individual life. Then since the soul is "the builder of the body," the deception which causes wrong thinking on the part of the intellectual man reproduces itself in physical imperfection and in adverse external circumstances.

What, then, is the deception which causes the "Fall"? This is figured by the Serpent. The serpent is a very favorite emblem in all ancient esoteric literature. It is sometimes used in a positive and sometimes in a negative sense. In either case it means life --- not the Originating Life-Principle, but the ultimate outcome of that Life-Principle in its most external form of manifestation. This, of course, is not bad in itself. Recognized in full realization of the fact that it comes from God, it is the completion of the Divine work by outward manifestation; and in this sense it becomes the serpent which Moses lifted up in the wilderness.

But without the recognition of it as the ultimate mode of the Divine Spirit (which is *all* that is), it becomes the deadly reptile, not lifted up, but crawling flat upon the ground: it is that ignorant conception of things which cannot see the spiritual element in them and therefore attributes all their energy of action and reaction to *themselves*, not perceiving that they are the creations of a higher power.

Ignorant of the Divine Law of Creation, we do not look beyond secondary causes; and therefore because our own creative thought-power is ever externalizing conditions *representative of our conceptions*, we necessarily become more and more involved in the meshes of a network of circumstances from which we can find no way of escape. How these circumstances come about we cannot tell. We may call it blind chance, or iron destiny, or inscrutable Providence; but because we are ignorant of the true Law of Primary Causation, we never suspect the real fact, which is that the originating power of all this in-harmony is ourself.

This is the great deception. We believe the serpent, that conception of life which sees nothing beyond secondary causation, and consequently we accept the Knowledge of Evil as being equally necessary with the Knowledge of Good; and so we eat of the tree of Knowledge of Good *and* of Evil. It is this dual aspect of knowledge that is deadly, but knowledge itself is nowhere condemned in Scripture; on the contrary, it is repeatedly stated to be the foundation of all progress. "Wisdom is a Tree of Life to them that lay hold upon her," says the Book of Proverbs.

But what is deadly to the soul of Man is the idea that Evil is a subject of Knowledge in and of itself just as Good is a subject of Knowledge. Therefore by thinking of Evil as a subject to be studied, we attribute to it a substantive existence of its own which it does not have. In other words, we look upon it as something having a self-originating power, and so, by the Law of the creative working of Thought, we bring the Evil into existence.

But this knowledge of our thought-action is not reached in the earlier history of the human race or of the individual, for the simple reason that all evolution takes place by Growth; and consequently if the reader realizes how this expulsion resulted from the Psychic intellectual Principle accepting Evil as a subject of Knowledge, he will now be able to understand certain further facts. We are told that the Lord God said, "Behold the man is become as one of us to know both good and evil," and then lest he put forth his hand and take of the tree of life and eat and live forever, the Lord God sent him out from the Garden of Eden" (Gen. 3:22-23). Looked at superficially, this seems like jealousy that man should have attained the same knowledge as God, and fear lest he should take the further step that would make him altogether God's equal. But such a reading of the text is babyish and indicates no conception of God as Universal All-originating Spirit, and we must therefore look for some deeper interpretation.

Now the deception into which Eve falls is attributing to Evil the same self-existence as to Good. There is no such thing as Evil in and of itself; and what we recognize as Evil is the ONE Good Power working as Disintegrating Force, because *we have not yet learned to direct it is such a way that it shall perform the functions of transition to higher degrees of Life without any disintegration of our individuality either in person or circumstances.* It is this disintegrating action that makes the ONE Power *appear* evil relatively to ourselves; and, so long as we conceive ourselves thus related to it, it does look as though it were balancing in itself the two opposite forces of Life and Death, Good and Evil, and it is in this sense that "God" is said to know both good and evil.

But this is a conception very different from that of the All-productive ONE and arises, not from the true nature of Being, but from our own confused Thought. But because the action of our Thought is always creative, the mere fact of our regarding Evil as an affirmative force in itself makes it so *relatively to ourselves*; and therefore no sooner do we fear evil than we begin to create the evil that we fear. To extinguish evil, we must learn not to fear it, and that means to cease recognizing it as having any power of its own; and so our salvation comes from realizing that in truth there is nothing but the good. But this knowledge can only be attained through long experience, which will at last bring Man to the place where he is able to deduce Truth from *a* principle prior to a conception of good and bad and to learn that his past experiences of evil have proceeded from his own inverted conceptions and are not founded upon Truth but upon its opposite.

Now lets glance briefly at the sentences pronounced upon the man, the woman, and the serpent. The serpent, in this connection being the principle of error which results in Death, can never come into any sort of reconciliation with the Divine Spirit, which is Truth and Life, and therefore the only possible pronouncement upon the serpent is a sentence of destruction. The penalty to Adam, or rather the physical body, is that of having to earn his bread by toilsome labor. This would not have been necessary if he had learned that his past experiences of evil proceeded from his own inverted conceptions and were not founded upon Truth but upon its opposite. If it were possible for him to live forever before gaining this experience, the result would be an immortality of misery, and therefore the Law of Nature renders it impossible for him to reach the knowledge which would place immortality within his grasp until he has gained that deep insight into the true working of causation which is necessary to make Eternal Life a prize worth having. For these reasons, man is represented as being expelled from Eden lest he should eat of the Tree of Life and live forever.

"This story of Eden is about each of us." The great Truth concerning Man is that he is the image and likeness of God. Man is ignorant of this Truth, this ignorance is his Fall. When he comes into the perfect knowledge of this Truth, this knowledge is his Rising-again; and these principles will expand until they bring us to the full Expression of the heavenly kingdom within us.

## Chapter 3
## ISRAEL

### The Patriarchs Abraham, Isaac, and Jacob

We are here in the transition stage from allegory to history.

I will not, however, here open the question whether the three Patriarchs were actual personages or, as some critics tell us, were merely the legendary ancestors of certain groups of wandering tribes. The frequency with which God is called in Scripture the God of Abraham, of Isaac, and of Jacob shows that something more must be referred to than the mere fact that the ancestors of the Jews worshipped Him, and the consideration of some of the prominent points in the history of these allegorical personages will throw a light on the subject which will be very helpful in our further investigation.

### Jacob and Personal Struggle

If we realize the truth, that the real object of the Bible is to convey the history of the spiritual Israel under the figure of Israel after the flesh, we shall see that the descent of Israel from the three Patriarchs must be a spiritual descent, and we may therefore expect to find in the Patriarchs themselves a fore-shadow of the principles which give rise to the spiritual Israel. Now we should particularly notice that the name "Israel" was bestowed on Jacob, the third Patriarch, on the occasion when he wrestled with an angel and as the result of his successful wrestling he obtained this name. We are told that Jacob recognized that it was the Divine Being, the Nameless ONE, with whom he wrestled, and this at once gives us the key to the allegory; for we know from the Master's instructions to the woman of Samaria that God is Universal Spirit. Under the figure, therefore, of wrestling with "an angel," we perceive that what Jacob wrestled with was the great problem of his own relation to the Universal Spirit allegorically represented as a powerful angel; and he held on and wrestled till he gained the blessing and the New Name in which the nature of that blessing was summed up. The conditions are significant. He was alone. Although he was the father of a large family none of his dear ones could help him in the struggle. We must each solve the problem of our relation to the Infinite Mind for ourselves; and not our nearest and dearest can wrestle for us.

And the struggle takes place in the darkness. It is when we begin to find that the light we thought we possessed is not the true light, when we find that its illuminating power is gone, that we rise nerved with an energy we never knew before and commence in earnest the struggle for the true Light, determined never to let go until we win the victory. And so we wrestle till the day begins to break, but even then we must not quit our hold; we must not be content until we have received the New Name which marks our possession of that principle of Light and Life which will forever expand into brighter day and fuller livingness.

But Jacob carries with him the mark of the struggle throughout his earthly career. The angel touched the hollow of his thigh, and thenceforward he was lame. The meaning is simple enough to those who have had some experience of the wrestling. They can never again walk in earthly things with the same step as before. They have seen the Truth, and they can never again un-see it; their whole standpoint has been altered and is no longer understood by those around them; to those who have not wrestled with the angel, they appear to walk lamely.

What, then, was the New Name that was thus gained by the resolute wrestler? His original name of Jacob was changed to Israel. The definition of Israel given in the seventy-third Psalm is "such as are of a clean heart," and Jesus expressed the same idea when he said, "Behold an Israelite indeed in whom is no guile," for the emphasis laid upon the word "Israelite" at once suggests some inner meaning.

The great fact about the spiritual Israel is therefore cleanness of heart and absence of guile --- in other words, perfect sincerity, which again implies singleness of purpose in the right direction. This, then, is the distinctive characteristic which attaches to the name of Israel, for it is this concentration of effort that is the prime factor in gaining the victory which leads to the acquisition of the Name. This is fundamental, and without it nothing can be accomplished; it indicates the sort of mental character which we must aim at, but it is not the meaning of the Name itself.

The name of Israel is composed of three syllables, each of which carries a great meaning. The first syllable, "Is," is primarily the sound of the in-drawing of the breath, and hence acquires the significance of the Life-Giving-Principle in general, and more particularly of the female individual Life. Hence the general conception conveyed by the syllable "Is" is that of a feminine spiritual principle manifesting itself in individuality --- that is to say, the "Soul" or formative element --- and it is thus indicative of all that we mean when we speak of the psychic side of nature.

Is--"Ra"--el

The second syllable, "Ra", is the name of the great Egyptian sun-god and is the complementary of everything that is signified by "Is." It is primarily indicative of physical life rather than psychic life. "Ra" symbolizes the masculine element as "Is" symbolizes the feminine.

Is--re--"El"

The third syllable, "El", has the significance of Universal Being. It is --- "The Nameless Principle" --- which includes in itself both the masculine and feminine elements, both the physical and the psychic, and is greater than them and gives rise to them. It is another form of the word "Most-High", and is indicative of the Supreme Principle before it passes into any differentiated mode. It is pure Spirit in the universal.

Now, if Man is to attain liberty, it can only be by the realization of these Three Modes of Being --- the physical, the psychic, and the spiritual; or, as the Bible expresses it, Body, Soul, and Spirit. He must know what these three are in himself and must also recognize the Source from which they spring, and he must at least have some moderately definite idea of their genesis into individuality. Therefore the man "instructed unto the kingdom of heaven" combines a threefold recognition of himself and of God which is accurately represented by the combination of the three syllables Is, Ra, and El.

Unless these three are joined into a single unity, a single word, the recognition is incomplete and the full knowledge of truth has not been attained. "Ra" by itself implies only the knowledge of the physical world, and results in Materialism. "Is" by itself realizes only the psychic world, and "El" by itself corresponds only with a vague apprehension of some overruling power, capricious and devoid of the element of Law, and thus results in idolatry.

This, then, was the significance of the New Name given to Jacob. He had wrestled with the Divine until the light had begun to dawn upon him, and he thus acquired the right to a name which should correctly describe what he had now become

## The Law of Three

We see, then, in the name of Israel the announcement of the three great principles into which all forms of manifestation must unite into a single Unity, and thus learn to form the name "Israel"; and in so doing we discover that it has now become our own name, for we find that the kingdom of heaven --- the realm of eternal principles --- is within us, and that, therefore, whatever we discover *"there"* is that which we ourselves *"are"*. Then our wrestling ceases: the Divine Wrestler has put his name upon us, and the day is beginning to dawn; but as yet it is only the earliest hour of daybreak; it is the true sunlight, but it is still low on the horizon, and we must not make the mistake of supposing that this early morning hour is the same as the mid-day glory --- in other words, we must not suppose that because we have once and forever finished wrestling with an unknown antagonist in darkness, therefore we have nothing more to do.

### Growth

Life is a perpetual doing, but, thank God, not a perpetual wrestling. It is exactly in proportion as we expand our doing that we expand our livingness. No one can grow for us, and it all depends upon ourselves how rapidly and how strongly we shall grow.

## Chapter 4
## THE MISSION OF MOSES

### Repetition of Principles

We have seen that the Bible teaching regarding Man starts with two great facts: first, that he is the image of God, thus Possessing God's Creative Process of Thought; and secondly, that he is ignorant of this truth, and so brings upon himself all sorts of trouble and limitation; and it is the purpose of this interpretation of the Bible to lead us step by step out of this ignorance into this knowledge. I say step by step, for it is a process of growth, first in the individual, then in the race, and this growth depends on certain clear and ascertainable Laws inherent in the constitution of Man. Now the peculiarity of inherent Law is that it always acts uniformly, making no exception in favor of anyone, and it does this as well positively as negatively.

### Ignorant Obedience

Our ignorance of any Law of Nature will never exempt us from its operation, and this is as true of ignorant obedience as of ignorant disobedience: the natural reward of ignorant obedience is no less certain than the natural punishment of ignorant disobedience; and it is on this principle that the great leaders of the race have always worked. They themselves knew the Law; but to impart the understanding of the Law to people in general was not the work of a day, nor of a generation, nor of many generations --- in fact it is a work which is still only in its infancy --- and therefore if people were to be saved from the consequences of disobedience to the Law, it could only be by some method of training which would lead them into ignorant obedience to it.

But this was not to be done by making any false statement of the Law, for Truth can never come out of falsehood; it must be done by presenting the Truth under such figures as would indicate the real relations of things, though not explaining how these relations arise, because to undeveloped minds such an explanation would be worse than useless. Hence came the whole system of the Mosaic Law.

## ONE Spirit

On one occasion, when the Master was asked which was the greatest commandment of the Law, he replied by quoting the fourth verse of the sixth chapter of Deuteronomy, "Hear, O Israel: the Lord our God is one Lord", or, as the Revised version has it in Mark 12:29, "the Lord is ONE". This, he says, is the first of all the commandments; and we may therefore expect to find in this statement of Divine Unity the foundation on which everything else rests. Nor need we look far to find the reason of it, for we have already seen in the opening words of Genesis that --- as the originating principle in all things --- there can be nothing else but God or Spirit. That is a conclusion which becomes unavoidable if we simply follow up the chain of cause and effect until we reach a Universal First Cause. We may call it by what name we choose: that will make no difference so long as we realize what must be its inherent nature and what must be our necessary relation to it.

This is the great Truth on which the mission of Moses was founded, and therefore that mission starts with the announcement of the Divine Name at the Burning Bush. Moses said unto God, Behold, when I come to the children of Israel, and shall say unto them, The God of your fathers hath sent me unto you; and they shall say to me, What is his name? what shall I say unto them? And God said unto Moses, I AM THAT I AM; and He said, Thus shalt thou say unto the children of Israel, I AM hath sent me unto you.

*So the name after which Moses inquired turned out to be no name, but the first person singular of the present tense of the verb TO BE, in its indicative mode.* **It is** *the announcement of **BEING** in the Absolute, in that first originating plane of Pure Spirit where, because the Material does not yet exist, there can be no extension in space, and consequently no sequence in time, and where therefore the only possible mode of being is the consciousness of Self-existence without limitation either of space or time, the realization of the "universal Here and the everlasting Now," the concentration of the All into the Point and the expansion of the Point into the All.* [For a fuller explanation of space and time, see the eleventh chapter of "The Essential THOMAS TROWARD".]

### The Egyptian Connection

But though this may have been a new announcement to the masses of the Hebrew people, it could have been no new announcement for Moses, for we are told in the Acts that Moses was learned in all the wisdom of the Egyptians, a circumstance which is fully accounted for by his education at the court of Pharaoh, where he would be as a matter of course initiated into the deepest mysteries of the Egyptian religion. He must therefore have been familiar from boyhood with the words, "I AM that I AM", which as the inscription "Nuk pu Nuk" appeared on the walls of every temple; and having received the highest instruction in the land, brought up as the son of Pharaoh's daughter, he must have been well aware of their significance. But this instruction had hitherto been confined to those in elevated positions.

In whatever way we may interpret the story of Moses' meeting with the Divine Being at the burning bush, one thing is evident: it indicates the point in his career when it became plain to him that the only possible way for the Liberation of mankind was through the universal recognition of that Truth which till now had been the exclusive secret of the elevated. What, then, was the great central Truth which was thus announced in this proclamation of the Divine Name? It has two sides to it. First, that Pure Spirit is the ultimate essence of all that is, and as a consequence the All-presence, the All-knowledge, the All-livingness, and the All-lovingness of "God" is in all things. Then as the corollary of the proposition that "Spirit is all that is", there must be the converse proposition that "all that "is" is Spirit"; and since Man is included in the "all", we are again brought back to the original description of him as spirit in the image and likeness of God.

But in those days people had to be educated up to these two great truths, and they have not advanced very far in this education yet; so from the time when Moses' eyes were opened to see in these truths not a secret to be guarded for his private benefit, but the power which was to expand to the renovation of the world, he realized that it was his mission to set men free by educating them gradually into the true knowledge of the Divine Name. Then he conceived a great scheme.

## The Mysteries and Religion

Modern research has shown us that the knowledge of this great fundamental truth was not confined to Egypt, but formed the ultimate center of all the religions of ancient times; it was that secret in which the supreme initiation of all the highest mysteries culminated. It could not be otherwise, for it was the only ultimate conclusion to which generations of clear-headed thinkers could come. But these were sages, priests, philosophers, men of education and leisure; and this final deduction was beyond the reach of the toiling multitudes, whose whole energies had to be devoted to the earning of their daily bread.

Still it was impossible for these thinkers who had arrived at the great knowledge to pass over the multitudes without allowing them at least a few crumbs from their table. The true recognition of the "Self" must always carry with it the purpose of helping others to acquire it also; but it does not necessarily imply the immediate perception of the best means of doing so, and hence *throughout ancient times we find an inner religion, the Supreme Mysteries, for the initiated few; and an outer religion, for the most part idolatrous, for the people. The people were not to be left without any religion, but they were given a religion which was deemed suited to their gross apprehension of things*; and in the hands of lower orders of priests --- themselves little, if at all, better instructed than the worshippers, these conceptions often became very gross indeed.

## National Calamity

*Moses saw that the* supreme secret of the Mysteries must be made the starting-point of the people's education; and therefore the mission to Israel must open with the declaration of the I AM as the All-embracing ONE.

A sentence consists of a subject and predicate, but in the announcement of the Divine Name made to Moses there is no predicate. The reason is that to predicate anything of a subject implies some special aspect of it, and thus by implication limits it, however extensive the predicate may be, and it is impossible to apply this mode of statement to the Universal Living Spirit. There can be nothing outside it. *"Itself"* is the Substance and the Life of all that is or ever can be. That is an ultimate conception from which it is impossible to get away from.

Therefore, the only predicate corresponding to the Universal Subject must be the enumeration of the innumerable --- the statement of all that is contained in infinite possibility --- and, consequently, the place of the predicate must be left apparently unfilled, because it is the fullness which includes all. The only possible statement of the Divine is that of Present Subjective Being, the Universal "I" and the ever-present "AM". Therefore I AM is the Name of God; and the First of all the Commandments is the announcement of the Divine Being as the Infinite ONE.

For more on the subject of the Unity of Spirit you can go to *chapter 11 of "The Essential THOMAS TROWARD"*, but I may repeat here the truth that, mathematically, the Infinite must be Unity. We cannot think of two Infinites, for as soon as duality appears, each member of it is limited by the other, else there would be no duality. Therefore we cannot multiply the Infinite. Similarly, we cannot divide it, for division again implies multiplicity or Numbers, and though these may be conceived of as existing relatively to each other within the Infinite, the very relation between them establishes limits where one begins and the other ends, and thus we are no longer dealing with the Infinite.

Of course all this is self-evident to the mathematician, who at once sees the absurdity of attempting to multiply or divide Infinity; but the non-mathematical reader should endeavor to realize the full meaning of the word "Infinite" as that which, being without limits, necessarily occupies all space and therefore includes all that is. The announcement that God is ONE is, therefore, the mathematical statement of the Universal Presence of Spirit, and the phrase "I AM" is the grammatical statement of the same thing.

And because the Universal Spirit is the Universal Life Itself, "over all, through all, and in all", there is yet a third statement of it, which is its Living statement: the reproduction of it in all things as well as man himself; and these three statements are one and cannot be separated. Each implies the two others, like the three sides of an equilateral triangle, and therefore the First of all the Commandments is that we shall recognize THE ONE. *As numerically all other numbers are developed from the unit number one,* so all the possibilities of ever-expanding Life are developed from the All-including UNIT of Being, and therefore in this Commandment we find the root of our future growth to all eternity. This is why both Moses and Jesus assign to it the supreme place.

## Moses and Jesus

And here let me point out the intimate relation between the teaching of Jesus and the teaching of Moses. They are the two great figures of the Bible. As the Old Testament centers round the one, so the New Testament centers round the other. Each appeals to the other. Moses says, "Of thy brethren, shall the Lord thy God raise up a prophet like unto me" --- the prophet that was to come should duplicate Moses; and when the prophet came, he said, "If they hear not Moses and the prophets, neither will they be persuaded by me". Each is the complement of the other. We shall never understand Jesus until we understand Moses, and we shall never understand Moses until we understand Jesus. Yet this is not a paradox, for to grasp the meaning of either we must find the key to their utterances in our own hearts and on our own lips in the words "I AM"; that is, we must go back to that Divine Universal Law of Being which is written within us, and of which both Moses and Jesus were the inspired exponents.

The mission of Moses, then, was to build up a nationality which should be independent both of time and country, and which should derive its solidarity from its recognition of the principle of THE ONE. Its national being must be based upon its expanding realization of the great central Truth, and to the guarding and development of that Truth this nation must be consecrated; and in the enslaved but not subdued children of the desert --- the children of Israel --- Moses had the material which he needed. For these wanderers, *without realizing it*, had brought with them a simple monotheistic creed, a belief in the God of Abraham, Isaac, and Jacob, which, vaguely though it might be, already touched the threshold of the sacred mystery. Here, then, Moses found the nucleus for the nationality he wanted to found, and so he led forth the people in that great symbolic march through the wilderness whose story is told in the Exodus.

To the details of that history we may turn more intelligently after we have gained a clearer idea of what the great work really was which Moses inaugurated on the night of the first Passover. Perhaps some of my readers may be surprised to learn that it is still going on and that they are called upon to take a personal part in continuing the work of Moses, which has now so expanded as to reach themselves. But all this is contained in the commission which Moses first announced to those he was to deliver and grows naturally out of its unfoldment. The name of the New Nation he was to lead has been accurately translated into "Israel", and the people led forth by Moses were proclaimed by the very terms of his commission to be "The People of the I AM".

Now the history of this people is dignified by a succession of Prophets such as no other nation lays claim to; yet the great Prophet who first consolidated their scattered tribes into a compact community, in prophesying the future of the people he had founded, passes over all these and, looking down the long centuries, points only to one other Prophet "like unto me". We constantly miss those little indications of Scripture on which the fuller understanding of it so greatly depends; and just as we miss the point when we are told that Man is created in the likeness of God, so we miss the point when we are told that this other prophet, Jesus, is a prophet of the same type as Moses.

The whole line of intervening prophets were not of that type. They had their own special work, but it was not a work like that of Moses. Isaiah, Jeremiah, Ezekiel, and the rest sink out of sight, and the only Prophet whom Moses sees in the future is brought into his field of vision by his likeness to himself. Any child in a Sunday school, if asked what he knew about Moses, would answer that he brought the children of Israel out of Egypt. No one would question that this was the distinctive fact regarding him, and therefore if we are to find a Prophet of the same type as Moses, we should expect to find in him the founder of a New Nationality of the same order as that founded by Moses --- that is to say, a nationality subsisting independently of time and place and cohering by reason of its recognition of an Eternal Ideal.

### I AM - - Therefore WE ARE

To make Jesus a Prophet like unto Moses, he must in some way repeat the Exodus and re-establish "the people of the I AM". Now turning to the teaching of Jesus, we find that this is exactly what he did. There was nothing on which he laid greater stress than the I AM. "Except ye believe that I AM, ye shall perish in your sins" was the emphatic summary of his whole teaching. And here read carefully. Distinguish between what Jesus said and what the translators of our English Bible say that he said, for it makes all the difference. Our English version runs, "If ye believe not that I am *He*, ye shall die in your sins" (John 8:24), thus, by the introduction of the single word "He" brought on the assuming of all sorts of theological doctrines of which would require a volume to itself. Not false doctrines, as such, but notions that convey limiting conceptions of ideals which could transcend all limitations. Thus, because both as theologians and grammarians the translators of the Authorized Version felt the want of a predicate to complete the words I AM, they added the word "he"; but, faithful according to their light, they were careful to draw attention to the fact that there was no "he" in the original, and therefore that word is printed in italics to show that it was supplied by the translators; and the Revised Version carefully notes this fact in the margin.

In the parallel case of the announcement to Moses at the burning bush, the translators did not attempt to introduce any predicate; they felt what I have pointed out: that no predicate could be sufficiently extensive to define Infinite Being; but here, supposing that Jesus was speaking of himself personally, they thought it necessary to introduce a word which should limit his statement accordingly. Now the only comment to be made on this passage of the English Bible is to note carefully that it is exactly what Jesus never said. In this connection he made no personal application of the verb "to be". What he said was, "Except ye believe that I AM, ye shall die in your sins" (R.V.). Now, if the criterion by which we are to recognize him as the Prophet predicted by Moses is his reproduction of the doings of Moses, then we cannot be wrong in supposing that his use of the I AM was as complete a generalization as was employed by Moses.

On the same principle on which theologians or grammarians would particularize the words to the individuality of Jesus, they might particularize them to Moses also. But going back to that generalized statement of Man which is the very first intimation the Bible gives of him, we find that if I AM is the generalized statement of "God", it can and must also be the generalized statement of "Man", for man is the image and likeness of God; so that whatever is universal in God becomes individual in man.

If, then, Jesus was to duplicate the work of Moses, it could only be by taking as the foundation of his teaching the same statement of essential Being that Moses took as the foundation of his; and therefore we must look for a generic, and not for a specific, application of the I AM in his teaching also. And as soon as we do this, the veil is lifted and a power streams forth from all his instructions which shows us that it was no mere figure of speech when he said that the water which he should give would become, in each one who drank it, a well of water springing up into everlasting life. He came not to proclaim himself, but Man; not to tell us of his own Divinity separating him from the race and making him the Great Exception, but to tell us of our Divinity and to show in himself the Great Example of the I AM reaching its full personal expression in Man.

This Prophet is raised up "of our brethren", he is one of ourselves, and therefore he said, "The disciple when he is perfected shall be as his Master". It is the Universal I AM reproducing itself in the individuality of Man that Jesus would have us believe in. He is preaching nothing but the same old Truth with which the Bible begins, that Man is the image and likeness of God. He says, in effect, Make this recognition the center of your life and you have tapped the source of everlasting life; but refuse to believe it and you will die in your sins. Why? As a Divine vengeance upon you for daring to question a theology that some narrow-minded clergy applied to all men? Certainly not. Truth has a surer foundation than forms of words; it is deep down in the foundations of Being; and it is the failure to realize this Truth of Being in ourselves that is the refusal to believe in the I AM which must necessarily cause us to perish in our sins. It is not a theological vengeance, but the Law of Nature. Let us inquire, then, what this Law is.

## The Great Law

It is the great Law that, to live at all, we must primarily live in ourselves. No one can live for us. We can never get away from being the center of our own world; or, in scientific language, our life is essentially subjective. There could be no objective life without a subjective entity to receive the perceptions which the objective faculties convey to it; and since the receiving entity is ourself, the only life possible to us is that of living in our own perceptions. *Whatever we believe, does, for us, in very fact exist.* Our beliefs may be erroneous from the point of view of a happier belief, but this does not alter the fact that for ourselves our beliefs are our realities, and these realities must continue until some ground is found for a change in belief. And in turn, the subjective entity reacts upon the objective life, for if there is one fact which the advance of modern psychological science is making more clear than another it is that the subjective entity is "the builder of the body". And this is precisely what, on the information we have already gleaned from the Bible, it ought to be; for we have seen that the statement that man is the image of God can only be interpreted as a statement of his having in himself the same creative process of Thought to which alone it is possible to attribute the origin of anything. He is the image of God because he is the individualization of the Universal Mind at that stage of self-evolution in which the individual attains the capacity for reasoning from the seen to the unseen, and thus for penetrating behind the veil of outward appearances; so that, because of the reproduction of the Divine creative faculty in himself, the man's mental states or modes of Thought are bound to externalize themselves in his body and his circumstances.

This being the Law, we see that the more closely our conception of ourselves approximates to a broad generalization of the factors which go to make human personality, rather than that narrow conception which limits our notion of ourselves to certain particular relations that have gathered around us, the more fully we shall externalize this idea of ourselves. And because the idea is a generalization independent of any particular circumstance, it must necessarily externalize as a corresponding independence of circumstances; in other words, it must result in a control over conditions, whether of body or environment, proportioned to the completeness of our generalization.

The more perfect the generalization, the more perfect the corresponding control over conditions; and therefore to attain the most complete control, which means the most perfect Liberty, we need to conceive of ourselves as embodying the idea of the most perfect generalization. But complete generalization is only another expression for infinitude, and therefore we have again reached the point where it becomes impossible to attach any predicate to the verb "to Be"; and so the only statement which contains the whole Law of Man's Being is identical with the only statement which contains the whole of God's Being, and consequently I AM is as much the correct formula for Man as for God.

## Sin

But if we do not believe this and make it the center of our life, we must perish in our sins. The Bible defines "sin" as "the transgression of the Law", and Jesus' warning is that by transgressing the Law of our own Being, we shall die. It would carry me beyond the general lines of this book to discuss the question of what is here meant by "Death"; but it is definitely not everlasting damnation.

The transgression of which Jesus speaks is the transgression of the Law of the I AM in ourselves, the non-recognition of the fact that we are the image and likeness of God. This is the old original sin of Eve. It is the belief in Evil as a substantive self-originating power. We believe ourselves under the control of all sorts of evils having their climax in Death; but whence does the evil get its power? Not from God, for no diminution of Life can come from the Fountain of Life. And if not from God, then from where else? God is the ONLY BEING --- that is the teaching of the First Commandment --- and therefore whatever "is" is some mode of God; and if this be so, then although evil may have a relative existence, it can have no substantive existence of its own. It is not a Living Originating Power. God, the Good, alone is that; and it is for this reason that in the doctrine of THE ONE and in the statement of the I AM is the foundation of eternal individual Life and Liberty.

So then the transgression is in supposing that there is, or can be, any Living Originating Power outside the I AM. Let us once see that this is impossible, and it follows that evil has no more dominion over us and we are free. But so long as we limit the I AM in ourselves to the narrow boundaries of the relative and conditioned and do not realize that, personified in ourselves, it must by its very nature still be as unfettered as when acting in the first creation of the universe, we shall never pass beyond the Law of Death which we thus impose upon ourselves.

In this way, then, Jesus proved himself to be the Prophet of whom Moses had spoken. He made the recognition of the I AM the sole foundation of his work; in other words, he placed before men the same radical and ultimate conception of Being that Moses had done --- but with a difference. Moses elaborated this conception from the standpoint of the Universal; Jesus elaborated it from that of the Individual. The work of Moses must necessarily precede that of Jesus, for if the Universal Mind is not in some measure apprehended first, the individual mind cannot be apprehended as its image and reflection.

But it takes the teaching of both Moses and Jesus to make the complete teaching, for each is the complement to the other, and it is for this reason that Jesus said he came not to destroy the Law but to fulfill it. Jesus took up the work where Moses left off, and expanded Moses' initial conception of a people founded on the recognition of the Unity of God into its proper outcome of the conception of a people founded on the recognition of the unity of Man as the expression of the Unity of God. How can we doubt that this latter conception also was in the mind of Moses? Had it not been, he would not have spoken of the Prophet (Jesus) like unto himself that would come after him. The Prophet that would gather the "People of the I AM" not only from a single nation (Israel), but from every nation under heaven.

## Chapter 5
## THE MISSION OF JESUS

### Natural Selection

Hitherto, our study of the Bible has worked along the lines of great Universal Laws naturally inherent in the constitution of Man and thus applicable to all men alike; but now we must turn to that other line of an Exclusive Selection. This is not an arbitrary selection --- for that would contradict the very conception of the unchangeable Universal Law on which the whole Bible is founded --- but it is a process of "natural selection" arising out of the Law itself and results not from any change in the Law but from the attainment of an exalted realization of what the Law really is. The first suggestion of this process of separation is contained in the promise that the deliverance of the race should come through "the Seed of the Woman", for in contra-distinction to this "Seed" there is the seed of the Serpent; "I will put enmity between thy seed and her seed".

Now was there in these things any arbitrary selection? After due consideration, we shall find that there was not and that they arose out of the perfectly natural operation of mental laws working on the higher levels of Individualism, and the indications of this operation are given in the story of Cain and Abel. Abel was a keeper of sheep and Cain was a tiller of the earth, and if the reader will bear in mind what I said regarding the symbolic character of Bible personages and the metaphorical use of words, the meaning of the story will become clear.

### Reason, Emotion, and Volition

There is a great difference between animal and vegetable life: the one is cold and devoid of any apparent element of volition, the other has a flow of warm blood and a quality of Will; so that as symbols, the animal represents the emotional qualities in Man, while the vegetable, following a mere law of sequence without the exercise of individual choice, more fitly represents the purely logical processes of reasoning.

Now we all know that the first spring of action in any chain of cause and effect which we set going starts with some emotion, some manner of feeling, and not with a mere argument. Argument, a reasoning process, may cause us to change the standpoint of our feeling and to conceive that as desirable which at first we did not consider so; but at the end it is the recognition of a desire which is the one and only spring of action. It is, therefore, the feelings and desires that give the true key to our life, and not mere logical statements; and so if the feelings and desires are going in the right direction, we may be very sure that the logic will not be wrong in its conclusions, even though it may be blundering in its method. Take care of the heart, and the head will take care of itself.

This, then, is the meaning of the story of Cain and Abel. If we realize that the Universal Mind, as the All-pervading undistributed Creative Power, must be subjective mind, we shall see that it can only respond in accordance with the Law of subjective mind; that is to say, its relation to the individual mind must always be in exact correspondence to what the individual mind conceives of it. This is unequivocally stated in a passage which is twice repeated in Scripture: "With the pure Thou wilt show Thyself pure; and with the froward Thou wilt show Thyself froward" (Psalm 18:26 and 2 Sam. 22:27).

If, therefore, we grasp this Law of Correspondence, we shall see that the only conception of the Divine Mind which will really vitalize our souls with living and life-giving power is to realize it not merely as a tremendous force to be mapped out intellectually according to its successive stages of sequence --- though it is this also --- but above all things as the Universal Heart with which our own must beat in sympathetic vibration if we would attain the true development of that power the possession of which constitutes "the glorious liberty of the sons of God" [Rom. 8:21].

In all our operations we must always remember that the Creative Power is a process of feeling and not of reasoning. Reasoning analyzes and dissects; feeling evolves and builds up. The relation between them is that reasoning explains how it is that feeling has this power; and the more plainly we see why it should be so, the more completely we are delivered from those negative feelings which act destructively by the same law by which affirmative feelings work constructively.

The first requisite, therefore, for drawing to ourselves that creative action of the Universal Spirit, which alone can set us free from the bondage of Limitation, is to call up its response on the side of feeling; and unless this is done first, no amount of argument, mere intellectuality, can have the desired effect, and this is what is symbolically represented in the statement that God accepted Abel's offering and rejected Cain's. It is the veiled statement of the truth that the action of the intellect alone, however powerful, is not sufficient to move the Creative Power. This does not in the least mean that the intellectual process is hurtful in itself or unacceptable before God, but it must come in its proper order as joining with feeling instead of taking its place. When a mere cold rational thinking is substituted for hearty warmth of volition, then Abel is symbolically slain by Cain.

## Guidance and Protection

But the allegory goes further. It tells us that the particular animal which Abel offered was the sheep; and from this point onward we find the metaphor of the shepherd and the sheep recurring throughout Scripture, and the reason is that the relation between the Shepherd and the Sheep is peculiarly one of Guidance and Protection. Now this brings us to the point which we may call the *"Severance of the Way"*. When we realize the Unity of the I AM ---- the identity, that is, of the Self-recognizing Principle in the Universal and in the Individual --- we may form three conceptions of it: one according to which the Universal I AM is reduced to a mere unconscious force, which the individual mind can manipulate without any sort of responsibility; another, the converse of this, in which Volition remains entirely on the side of the Universal Mind, and the individual becomes a mere automaton; and the third, in which each phase of Mind is the reciprocal of the other, and consequently the motivation for action may commence on either side.

Now it is this reciprocal action that the Bible all along puts before us as the true Way. From the center of his own smaller circle of perception the individual is free to make any selection that he will, and if he acts from a clear recognition of the true relations of things, the first use he will make of this power will be to guard himself against any possible misuse of it by recognizing that his own circle revolves within the greater circle of that Whole of which he is an infinitesimal part; and therefore he will always seek to conform his individual action to the movement of the Universal Spirit.

His sense of the Wholeness of that Universal Life which finds Individual center in himself, and his consciousness of his identity with it, will lead him to see that there must be, above his own individual view of things derived from a merely partial knowledge, a higher and more far-seeing Wisdom which, because it is the Life-in-itself, cannot be in any way adverse to him; and he will therefore seek to maintain such a mental attitude as will draw towards himself the response of the Universal Mind as a Power of unfailing Guidance, Provision, and Protection. But to do this means the curbing of that self-will which is guided only by the narrow perception of expediency derived from past experiences; in other words, it requires us to act from trust in the Universal Mind, thus investing it with a Personal character, rather than from calculations based on our own objective view, which is necessarily limited to secondary causes. In a word, we must learn to walk by faith and not by sight.

## Sacrifice

Now the institution of Sacrifice was the most effective way for impressing this mental attitude upon the unlearned. Viewed merely superficially, it looks as if it is the desire of the worshipper to submit himself to the Divine Guidance by reconciliation through giving an offering to gain it's favor, but, it was actually meant to be a teaching tool to help maintain the required mental attitude until the unlearned reached the point where they could see that the Universal Mind, which is also the Universal LAW, cannot have a retrospective vindictive character any more than any of the Laws of nature which emanate from it. When we see that the true sacrifice is the willingness to give up smaller personal aims for the purpose of bringing into concrete manifestation those great principles of universal harmony which are the foundations of the Kingdom of God; when we reach this point; we see the philosophical reasons why the maintenance of this attitude of the individual towards the Universal Mind is the one and only basis on which the individuality can expand or, indeed, continue to exist at all.

It is in correspondence with these three stages that the Bible first puts before us the Levitical sacrifices, next explains these as symbols of the Great Sacrifice of the Suffering Messiah, and finally tells us that God does not require the death of any victim and that the true offering is that of the heart and the will; and so the Psalms sum up the whole matter by saying, "Sacrifice and burnt-offering thou wants not" [Ps. 40:6], and instead of these,

"Lo, I come to do Thy will, O my God; yea, Thy Law is within my heart" [Ps. 40:8].

## Covenant

Now the idea of Sacrifice and the idea of Covenant are naturally, or reciprocally, related. If the acceptance of the principle of Sacrifice brings the worshipper into a peculiarly close relation to the Divine Mind, it equally brings the Divine Mind into a peculiarly close relation to the worshipper; and since the Divine Mind is the Life-in-itself, the very Essence-of-Being which is the root of all conscious individuality, this identification of the Divine with the Individual results in his continual expansion, or, to use the Master's words, in his having Life and having it more abundantly [John 10:10]; and consequently, his powers steadily increase, and he is led by the most unlooked-for sequences of cause and effect into continually improving conditions which enable him to do more and more effectual work, so as to make him a center of power, not only to himself, but to all with whom he comes in contact.

This continual progress is the result of the natural law of the relation between himself and the Universal Mind when he does not invert its action, and because it works with the same unchangeableness as all other Natural Laws, it constitutes an Everlasting Covenant which can no more be broken than those astronomical laws which keep the planets in their orbits, the smallest infraction of which would destroy the entire cosmic system; and it is for this reason that we find in the Bible such frequent references to the Laws of Nature as typical of the certainty of the relation between God and His people. "Gather My People together unto Me; those that have made a covenant with Me by sacrifice" (Psalm 50:5); the two principles of Sacrifice and Covenant rightly understood will always be found to go hand in hand.

The idea of Guidance and Protection which is thus set forth recurs throughout the Bible under the emblem of the Shepherd and the Sheep, and it is in a peculiar manner appropriated to "the People of the I AM": "From thence is the Shepherd, the Stone of Israel" (Gen. 49:24). In other passages we hear; "Give ear, O Shepherd of Israel", (Psalm 80:1); and "The Lord is my Shepherd; I shall not want" (Psalm 23:1); If, then, this conception of the Shepherd and the Sheep represents the mental attitude of "Israel", we may reasonably expect it to be precisely opposite to all that is symbolically meant by "Egypt". If "Israel" takes for its Stone of Foundation the principle of Guidance by the Supreme Power, then "Egypt" must base itself on the contrary principle of making its own choice without any guidance --- that is to say, determined self-will. And hence we find it written that "every Shepherd is an abomination to the Egyptian" (Gen. 46:34).

## Subconscious Mind

Now it is a very remarkable thing that tradition points to the Great Pyramid as having been erected by a *"Shepherd"* power which dominated Egypt, not by force of arms, but by a mysterious influence which, although they detested it, the Egyptians found it impossible to resist. These *"Shepherds"* built the Great Pyramid and then, having accomplished their work, returned to the land from whence they came. So says the tradition. The Pyramid remains to this day, and the researchers of modern science show us that it is a monumental statement of all the great measures of the cosmic system wrought out with an accuracy which can only be accounted for by more than human knowledge.

And where should we find this knowledge except in the Universal Mind of which the cosmic system is the visible manifestation? Since this mind is primarily subconscious, then, by the general law of relation between subjective and objective mind, it can reproduce its inherent knowledge of all cosmic facts in any individual mind that has systematically trained itself into sympathy with the Universal Mind in that particular direction. But such training is impossible unless the individual mind first recognizes the Universal Mind as an Intelligence capable of giving the highest instruction, and to which, therefore, the individual mind is bound to look for guidance.

We must carefully avoid the mistake of supposing that subconscious-ness means unconsciousness. That idea is clearly proved wrong by hypnotism. Whatever unconsciousness there may be is on the part of the objective mind, which is unconscious of the action of the subjective mind. But a careful study of the subject shows that the subjective mind, so far from knowing less than the objective mind, knows infinitely more; and if this be true of the individual subjective mind, how much more must it be true of the Universal Subjective Mind, of which all individual consciousness is a particular mode of manifestation.

For these reasons, the only people who could build such a monument as a Great Pyramid must be those who realized the principles of Divine Guidance or the Power which is set forth under the emblem of the Shepherd and the Sheep; and therefore we can see how it is that tradition associates the building of the Pyramid with a Shepherd Power.

## Sacred Geometry

Nor is this all. Having first demonstrated its trustworthiness by the refined accuracy of its astronomical and geometric measurements, the Pyramid challenges our attention with a series of time-measurements, all of which were prophetic at the date of its erection, and some of which have already become historic, while the period of others is now rapidly running out. The central point of these time-measurements is the date of the birth of

Christ, and if we think of him in his character of "the Good Shepherd", we have yet another testimony to the supreme importance which Scripture attaches to the relation between the Shepherd and the Sheep. For the Great Pyramid is a Bible in stone, and there can be no doubt that it is this marvel of the ages which is referred to in the nineteenth chapter of Isaiah, where it says, "In that day there shall be an altar to the Lord in the midst of the land of Egypt". And so we find that the central fact to which the Great Pyramid leads up is the coming of "the Good Shepherd"; and Jesus explains the reason for this title in the fact that "the Good Shepherd giveth his life for the Sheep". That is what distinguishes him from the hireling who is not a true shepherd; so that here we find ourselves back again at the idea of Sacrifice, only now it is not the Sheep that are sacrificed but the Shepherd. Could anything be plainer? The sacrifice is not an offering of blood to a blood thirsty Deity, but it is the Chief Shepherd sacrificing himself to the necessities of the case.

And what are the necessities of the case? The student of Mental Science should see here the grandest application of the Law of Suggestion in a supreme act of self-devotion logically proceeding from the knowledge of the fundamental truths regarding Subjective and Objective Mind. Jesus stands before us as the Grand Master of Mental Science. It is written that "he knew what was in man" [John 2:25], and in his mission we have the practical fruits of that knowledge.

The Great Sacrifice is also the Great Suggestion. If we realize that the Creative Power of our Thought is the root from which all our experiences, whether subjective or objective, arise, we shall see that everything depends on the nature of the suggestions which give color to our Thought. If from our consciousness of guilt they are suggestions of retribution, then, in accordance with the predominating tone of our Thought, we shall externalize the evil that we fear; and if we carry this terrible suggestion with us through the gate of death into that other life which is purely subjective, then assuredly it will work itself out in our realizations, and so we must continue to suffer until we believe that we have paid the uttermost farthing. This is not a judicial sentence, but the inexorable working of Natural Law. But if we can find a counter-suggestion of such paramount magnitude as to obliterate all sense of liability to punishment, then, by the same Law, our fears are removed; and whether in the body or out of the body, we rejoice in the sense of pardon and reconciliation to our Father which is in heaven.

Now we can well imagine that one who has attained the supreme knowledge of all Laws, and as a consequence has developed the powers which the knowledge must necessarily carry with it, would find in the conveying of such an incalculably valuable suggestion to the race an object worthy of his exalted capacities, and if the Law of Suggestion was to be employed in such a way as to appeal to the whole race, it could only be by so deeply impressing them with the realization of the Divine Love that all fear should be forever cast out; therefore the suggestion must be that of a Love which nothing can exceed.

And herein is the difference between the crucifixion of Jesus and those thousands of other crucifixions which disgraced the annals of Rome: it was entirely voluntary. This also places it above all other acts of heroism. Many have died for the sake of others, and their devotion consisted in accepting it when and how they did. But with Jesus the case was entirely different. He was under no compulsion to do so; therefore his yielding himself to a death of excruciating agony was the master-stroke of Love and the supreme practical application of Mental Science; for the crude conception of the Father's "justice" being satisfied by the sacrifice of "the Son", however faulty both as Law and as Theology, in no way misses the mark from the metaphysical standpoint of Suggestion; and those who have not yet gotten beyond this stage in their conception of the Divine Being receive the assurance of the Divine Love towards themselves as completely as those who are able to grasp most clearly the sequence of cause and effect really involved; and for these latter it resolves itself into the simple argument, with still greater reason, that if the Universal Spirit could thus inspire one to die for us, then It cannot be less loving in the bulk than It has shown Itself in the sample.

## Universal Law in Practice

It is an axiom that the Universal cannot act on the plane of the Particular except by becoming individualized upon that plane, and therefore we may argue that so far as it was possible for the Universal Spirit to give Itself to death for us, It did so in the person of Jesus Christ; and so we may say that to all intents and purposes God died for us upon the Cross to prove to us the Love of God. Let us, then, no longer doubt the fact of this Love but, realizing it to the full, let us make the Cross of Christ not the mysterious end of an unintelligent religion, but the beginning of a bright, practical, and glorious New Life, taking for our starting-point the apostolic words, "there is now no condemnation to them that are in Christ Jesus" [Rom. 8:1]. We have now consciously left all condemnation behind us, and we set forward on our New Life with the self-obvious maxim that "if God be for us, who can be against us?" [Rom. 8:31] We may meet with opposition, but there is with us a Power and an Intelligence which no opposition can overcome, and so we become "more than conquerors through Him that loved us" (Rom. 8:37).

This is the nature of the Great Suggestion wrought out by Jesus; so that here again we find that the acceptance of the Great Sacrifice gives rise to the consciousness of a peculiarly close and endearing relation between the Individual and the Universal Mind, which may well be described as an Everlasting Covenant because it is founded not on any favoritism on the part of God, neither on any deeds of merit on the part of Man, but on the accurate working of Universal Law when realized in the higher manifestations of Individualism; and so it is truly written, "by his Knowledge shall My righteous servant justify many" [Is. 53:11]. Thus it is that Jesus completes the work of Moses in building up into a peculiar people, a chosen generation, "the People of the I AM" (1 Peter 2:9).

### Blood-Line and Inheritance

For the reasons which I have now endeavored to explain, the principle of "the Shepherd" is "the Stone of Israel". It is that great ideal by which the nationality of the "People of the I AM" coheres, and it is, therefore, at once the Foundation Stone and the Crowning Stone of the whole edifice. To those who cannot realize the great universal truths which are summed up in the twofold ideal of Sacrifice and Covenant, it must always be the Stone of stumbling and the Rock of offence; but to "the People of the I AM", whether individually or collectively, it must forever be "the Stone of Israel" [Gen 49:24] and "the Rock of our Salvation" [e.g. Ps. 95:1]. To lay in place this Chief Corner Stone was the mission of Jesus Christ.

## Chapter 6
## THE BUILDING OF THE TEMPLE

### Universal Principle

In our study of the Bible, we must always remember that, rightly interpreted, it is seeking to teach us the knowledge of the grand Universal principles which are at the root of all modes of living activity, whether in that world of environment which we commonly speak of as Nature, or in those human relations which we call the World of Man, or in those innermost springs of being which we speak of as the Divine World. The Bible is throughout dealing with those three factors, which I have spoken of in the commencement of this book as "God", "Man", and "the Universe", and is explaining the Law of Evolution by which "God" or Universal Undifferentiated Spirit continually passes into more and more perfect forms of Self-expression culminating in Perfected Man; And however deep the mysteries we may encounter, there is nothing unnatural anywhere. Everything has its place in the due order of the Great Whole. A mistaken conception of this Order may lead us to invert it, and by so doing we provide those negative conditions whose presence calls forth the Power of the Negative with all its disastrous consequences; but even this inverted action is perfectly natural, for it is all according to recognizable Law, whether on the side of calculation or of feeling.

These Laws of the Universe, whether within us or without or around us, are always the same, and the only question is whether through our ignorance we shall use them in that inverted sense which sums them all up in the Law of Death, or in that true and harmonious order which sums them up in the Law of Life. These are the things which under a variety of figures the Bible presents to us, and it is for us by reverent, yet intelligent, inquiry to penetrate the successive veils which hide them from the eyes of those who will not take the trouble to investigate for themselves. It is this Grand Order of the Universe that is symbolized by Solomon's Temple.

## From Moses Through Solomon to Jesus

We have seen that it was the mission of Moses to mold into definite form the material which ages of unnoticed growth had prepared, to consolidate into national being "the People of the I AM", and to lead them out of Egypt. This work, with which the truly national history of Israel commenced, had its completion in the reign of Solomon, when all enemies had been uprooted from the Promised Land, and the state founded by Moses out of wandering tribes had culminated in a powerful monarchy, ruled over by a king whose name has ever since become both in East and West the synonym for the supreme attainment of wisdom, power, and glory.

If the purpose of Moses had been only that of a national lawgiver and founder of a political state it would have found its perfect attainment in the reign of Solomon; but Moses had a far grander end in view, and looking down the long vista of the ages he saw, not Solomon, but the carpenter who said, "a greater than Solomon is here" (Matt. 12:42; Luke 11:31). And the way for the carpenter could only be prepared by that long period of corruption which set in with the first days of Solomon's successor. "The People of the I AM" are concealed among all nations and must be brought forth by the Prophet, who should realize the work of Moses not only in a national, but also in a universal, significance.

These are the three typical figures of Hebrew history; the beginning, the middle, and the end --- Moses, Solomon, Jesus; and the three are distinguished by one common characteristic: they are all Builders of the Temple. Moses erected the tabernacle, that portable temple which accompanied the Israelites in their journeyings. Solomon reproduced it in an edifice of wood and stone fixed firmly upon its rocky foundation. Jesus revealed it as the individual intellect.

## Builders

Thus they stand before us the Three Great Builders, each building with a perfect knowledge according to a Divine pattern; and if the Divine is that in which there is no variableness of shadow of turning (James 1:17), how can we suppose that the pattern was other than one and the same? We may, therefore, expect to find in the work of the three Builders the same principles, however differently expressed; for they each in different ways proclaimed the same all-embracing truth that God, Man, and the Universe, however varied may be the multiplicity of outward forms, are ONE. St Paul gives us an important key to the interpretation of Scripture when he tells us that its leading characters also represent great universal principles, and this is pre-eminently the case with Solomon. His name is derived from a word signifying Wholeness, and therefore means the man who has realized "the Wholeness", or in other words the Universal Unity. This is the secret of his greatness.

He who has found the Unity of the Whole has obtained "the Key of Knowledge", and it is now in his power to enter intelligently into the study of his own being and of the relations which arise out of it, and to help others as he himself advances into greater light. This is the man who is able to become a Builder. But such a man must be the "Son of David".

## Love

The Builder of the Temple, then, must be "the Son of David"; and again we find that much of the significance of this saying is concealed in the name. David is the English form of the Oriental name which means "Beloved", and the Builder is therefore the Son of the Beloved. David is called in Scripture "the man after God's own heart", a description exactly answering to the name; and we therefore find that Solomon the Builder is the son of the man who has entered into that reciprocal relation with "God", or the Universal Spirit, which can only be described as Love.

When this recognition by the individual mind of its own nature and of its relation to the Universal Mind takes place, it gives birth to a new being in the man; for he now finds not that he has ceased to be the self he was before, but that that self includes a far greater self, which is none other than the reproduction of the Universal Self in his individual consciousness. Thenceforward he works more and more from set purpose by means of this greater self, the self within the self, as he grows into fuller understanding of the Law by which this greater self has become developed within him.

He learns that it is this greater self within the self that is the true Builder, because it is none other than the reproduction of the Infinite Creative Power of the Universe. He realizes that the working of this power must always be a continual building up. It is the Universal Life-Principle, and to suppose that to have any other action than continual expansion into more and more perfect forms of self-expression would be to suppose it acting in contradiction to its own nature which, whether on the colossal scale of a solar system or on the miniature one of a man, must be that of a self-inherent activity which is forever building up.

When anyone is thus intellectually enlightened, he has reached that stage of development which is signified by the name David: he is "beloved" --- that is to say, he is exercising a specific individual attraction towards the Spirit in its universal and undifferentiated mode.

## Evolution

We are here dealing with the Principle of Evolution in its highest phases, and if we keep this in mind it becomes clear that the intellectual man who perceives this in himself is himself the evolving principle manifesting at that stage where it becomes an individuality capable of understanding its own identity with the Spiritual Force which, by Self-evolution, produces all things. He thus realizes himself to be the Reciprocal of the Universal Mind, which is the Divine Spirit, and he sees that his reciprocity consists in Evolution having reached in him the point where it cannot continue in its highest phases without the factor, namely, of his individual will. If we lose sight of this we lose the key to the whole teaching of the Bible. We must understand ***the Universal cannot, as such, initiate a course of action on the plane of the particular; It can do so only by becoming the individual which is precisely the production of the intellectually enlightened man we are now talking about***. The failure to see this very obvious Law is the root of all the theological discordances that have retarded the work of true religion to the present time, and therefore the sooner we see through the error, the better.

Anyone who has advanced to the perception of this Law necessarily becomes a center of attraction to Undifferentiated Spirit in its highest modes, the modes of Intelligence and Feeling, as well as in its lower modes of Vital Energy. This results from the very nature of the evolutionary Process. All creation commences with the primary movement of the Spirit, and since the Spirit is Life-in-itself, this movement must be forever going on.

This is exactly what Jesus said to the woman of Samaria: "The Father (Universal Spirit) seeketh such to worship Him [John 4:23]; and it is because of this mutual attraction between the individual mind that has come to the knowledge of its own true nature and the Universal Mind that the person who is thus enlightened is called "the Beloved"; he is beginning to understand what is meant by Man being the image of God and to grasp the significance of the old-world saying that "Spirit is the power that knows itself".

As this intellectual comprehension of the great truth matures, it gives rise to the recognition of an interior power which is something beyond the intellect but not yet independent of it, something regarding which we can make intellectual statements that clear the way for its recognition, but which is itself a Living Power and not a mere statement about such a power.

It may seem a truism to say that no statement about a thing is the thing, yet we are apt to miss this in practice. The Master pointed this out very clearly when he said to the Jews, "Search the Scriptures, for in them ye think ye have everlasting life, and they testify of Me" (John 5:39). He said in effect, "You make a mistake by supposing that the reading of a book can in itself confer Life. What your Scriptures do is to make statements regarding that which I am. Realize what those statements mean, and then you will see in me the living example of the Living Truth; and seeing this, you will seek for the development of the same thing in yourselves. The disciple, when perfected, shall be as his Master".

The Building-Power is that innermost spiritual faculty which is the reproduction in the individual of the same Universal Building-Power by which the whole Creation exists, and the purpose of intellectual statements regarding it is to remove mental obstacles and to induce the mental state which will enable this supreme innermost power to work in accordance with conscious selection on the part of the individual. It is the same power which has brought the race up to where it is, and which has evolved the individual as part of the race.

***All further evolution must result from the conscious employment of the Evolutionary Law by the intelligence of the individual himself.*** Now it is this recognized innermost creative power that is signified by Solomon --- it must be preceded by the purified and enlightened intellect --- and therefore it is called the Son of David, "the Beloved," and becomes the Builder of the Temple. For the Master's statement shows that, in its true significance, the Temple is that of Man's individuality; and if this is so with the individual, equally it must be so in the totality of manifested being, and thus it is also true that the whole Universe is none other than the Temple of the Living God.

### Symbolizing Divine Presence

This great truth of the Divine Presence is what the instructed builders sought to symbolize in Solomon's Temple, whether that Presence be considered on the scale of the Universe or of an individual man. If the Universal Divine Presence is a fact, then the Individual Divine Presence is a fact also, because the individual is included in the Universal; it is the working of a general Law in a particular instance, and thus we are brought to one of the great statements of the ancient wisdom, that Man is the Microcosm --- that is to say, the reproduction of all the principles which give rise to the manifestation of the Universe, or the Macrocosm; and therefore, to serve its proper symbolic purpose, the Temple must represent both the Macrocosm and the Microcosm.

It would be far too elaborate a work for the present volume to enter in detail into the symbolical statements of both the physical and supra-physical nature contained first in the Tabernacle and afterwards in the Temple; so let it suffice to say that as the

Universal Mind inspired the builders of the Pyramid with the correct knowledge of the cosmic measures, so the Bible tells us that Moses was inspired to produce in the Tabernacle the symbolic representation of great universal truths; he was bidden to make all things accurately according to the pattern showed him on the Mount, and the same truths received a more permanent symbolization in Solomon's Temple.

An excellent example of this symbolism is afforded by the two pillars set up by Solomon at the entrance to the Temple: the one on the right hand, called Jachin, and the one on the left, called Boaz (1 Kings 7:21). They seemed to have had no structural connection with the building but merely to have stood at its entrance for the purpose of bearing these symbolic names. What, then, do they signify? The English J often stands for the Oriental Y, and the name Jachin is therefore Yakhin, which is an intensified form of the word YAK or ONE, thus the Mathematical element of Unity throughout the Universe, since all numbers are evolved from the number ONE.

But the mathematical element is the element of Measurement, Proportion, and Relation. It is not the Living Life, but only the recognition of the proportional adjustments which the Life gives rise to. To balance the Mathematical element we require the Vital element, and this element finds its most perfect expression in that wonderful complex of Thought, Feeling, and Volition which we call Personality. The pillar Jachin is therefore balanced by the pillar Boaz, a name connected with the root of the word Voice.

Speech is the distinguishing characteristic of Personality. To clothe a conception in adequate language is to give it definition and thus make it clear to ourselves and to others. A distinct statement of our idea is the first step in the operation of consciously building it up into concrete existence, and therefore we find that in all the great religions of the race, the Divine Creative Power is spoken of as "the Word".

## "The Word" an Expression of Purpose

Let us get away from all confused mysticism regarding this term. The formulated Word is the expression of a definite Purpose, and therefore it stands for the action of Intelligent Volition; and it is as showing the place which this factor holds in the evolutionary process that the pillar Boaz stands opposite the pillar Jachin as its necessary compliment and balancing factor. The union of the two signifies Intelligent Purpose working by means of the Necessary Law, and the only way of entering into "the Temple," whether of the cosmos or of the individual, is by passing between these Two Pillars of the Universe, and realizing the combined action of Law and Volition.

This is the Narrow Way that leads us into the building not made with hands, within which all the mysteries shall be unfolded before us in a regular order and succession. He who climbs up some other way is a thief and a robber, and brings punishment upon himself as the natural effect of his own rashness, for knowing nothing of the *true* Order of the Inner Life, he plunges prematurely into the midst of things of whose real nature he is ignorant, and sooner or later learns through pain and suffering the cost of such foolishness.

We may not enter the Temple save by passing between the pillars, and we cannot pass between them till we can tell their meaning. It is the purpose of the Bible, rightly interpreted, to give us the Key to this Knowledge; it is not the only instruction it has to give, but it is the initial course, and when this has been mastered it will open out deeper things, the inner secrets of the sanctuary. But the first thing is to pass between Jachin and Boaz, and then the Divine Interpreter will meet us on the threshold and will unfold the mysteries of the Temple in their due order, so that as each one is opened to us in succession, we are prepared for its reception and thus need fear no danger, because at each step we always know what we are dealing with and have attained the spiritual, intellectual, and physical development qualifying us to employ each new revelation in the right way.

For the opening of the inner mysteries is not for the gratification of mere idle curiosity; it is for the increasing of our Livingness; and the highest quality of Livingness is Life-givingness; and every measure of Life-givingness, be it only the giving of a cup of cold water (Matt. 10:42) means use of the powers and knowledge which we possess. The Temple instruction is therefore intended to qualify us as workers, and the value to ourselves of what we receive within is seen in the measure of intelligence and love with which we transmute our Temple gold into the current coin of daily life.

**"The Stone"**

The building-up process is that of Evolution, whether in the material world or in the human individuality or in the race as a whole, and the Bible presents the analogy to us very forcibly under the metaphor of "the Stone". Speaking of the rejection of his own teaching, the Master said, "What is this, then, that is written, 'The Stone which the builders rejected, the same is become the head of the corner'?" referring to the 118th Psalm (Luke 20:17). A careful perusal of the Master's history as given in the Gospel will show us very clearly what *"the Stone is"*; it is the material out of which the Temple of the Spirit is to be built up, which we now see is nothing else than *Perfected Humanity*.

Each individual is a temple himself, as St Paul tells us, and at the same time a single stone in the construction of the Great Temple which is the regenerated race, that "People of the I AM" which was inaugurated when Moses first pitched the tabernacle in the wilderness. But the process must always be an individual one, for a nation is nothing but an aggregation of individuals, and therefore in considering the metaphor of "the Stone" as applied to the individual, we shall realize its wider application also.

Now the Master was tried by a Jewish council and sentenced to execution on the charge of blasphemy for asserting the identity of his own nature with that of God, but because the Jews were subject to Roman rule, which forbid then to execute anyone, it became necessary to substitute for the original charge of blasphemy one of high treason, so as to bring it within the jurisdiction of the *Roman* court, "Whosoever maketh himself a king speaketh against Caesar" (John 19:12) --- and so the inscription fastened to the cross was "Jesus of Nazareth, the King of the Jews" (John 19:19). But the true reason why Jesus was hunted to death was expressed by the Jewish scribes who mocked the sufferer with the words "He trusted in God; let Him deliver him now if He will have him, for he said 'I am the son of God'." (Matt. 27:43)

The teaching of Jesus was the inversion of all that was taught by the official priesthood. Their whole teaching rested on the hypothesis that God and Man are absolutely distinct in nature, thus directly contradicting the earliest statement of their own Scriptures regarding Man, that he is the image and likeness of God. As a consequence of this false assumption, they supposed that the whole Mosaic Law and Ritual was intended to pacify God and make him favorable to the worshipper, and so in their minds the entire system tended only to emphasize the gulf that separated Man from God.

## Cause and Effect

What the connection of cause and effect was by which this system operated to produce the result of reconciling God to the worshipper was a question which they never attempted to face; for had they, after the example of their patriarch Jacob, determinedly wrestled with the problem of why their Law was what it was, that Law would have shone forth with a self-illuminating light which would have made clear to them that all the teaching of Moses and the Prophets and the Psalms was concerning that grand ideal of a Divine Humanity which it was the mission of Jesus to proclaim and exemplify.

But they would not face the question of the reason for these things. They had received a certain traditional interpretation of their Scriptures and their Ritual and, as Jesus said, made the real commands of God void by their traditions. They did not inquire what Moses meant, but only followed on the lines of what "authorities" said he meant; in other words, they would not think for themselves. They were content to say, "Our Law and Ritual are what they are because God has so ordered them"; but they would not go further and inquire why God ordered them so.

With them, the whole question of revelation became the question whether Moses had or had not made such an announcement of the Divine Will, and so their religion rested ultimately only on historical evidences. But they did not face the question, "How am I to know that the so-called prophet ever received any communication from the Divine at all?" In the last resort, there can be only one criterion by which to judge the truth of any claim to a Divine communication, which is that the message should present an intelligible sequence of cause and effect.

## Truth

No man can prove that God has spoken to him; the only possible proof is the inherent truth of the message, making it appeal to our feelings and our reason with a power that carries conviction with it. "The Spirit of Truth shall convince you", said the Master; and when this inner conviction of Truth is felt, it will invariably be found that, by thinking it over carefully, the reason of the feeling will manifest itself in an intelligible sequence of cause and effect. Short of realizing such a sequence, we have not realized the Truth. The only other proof is that of practical results, and to this test the Master tells us to bring the teaching that we hear; and the teaching he bade us judge by this standard was his own. It is a principle that no great system can endure for ages, exercising a widespread and permanent influence over large masses of mankind, without any element of Truth in it. There have been, and still are, great systems influencing mankind which contain many and serious errors, but what has given them their power is the Truth that is in them and not the error; and careful inquiry into the secret of their vitality will enable us to detect and remove the error.

Now had the leaders of the Jews investigated their national system with intelligence and moral courage, they would have determined that its manifest vitality and elevating spiritual tone showed that it contained a great and living Truth. This Truth could not be in the mere external observances and the promised results, and therefore the vitalizing Truth must be in some principle which supplied the connection that was apparently wanting. They would have determined that God could not have arbitrarily commanded a set of meaningless observances, and that therefore these observances must be the expression of some LAW inherent in the very nature of Man's being.

In a word, they would have realized that, to be true at all, a thing must be within the All-embracing Law of Cause and Effect, and that religion itself could be no exception to the rule --- it must, in short, be natural because, if God be ONE, He cannot introduce anywhere an arbitrary or uncertain principle of Order throughout the Universe. To suppose the introduction of anything by a mere act of Divine Volition, without a foundation in the sequence of the Universal Order, would be to deny the Unity of God, and thus to deny the Divine Being altogether.

Had the rulers of Israel, therefore, understood the meaning of the first two Commandments, they would have realized that their first duty, as instructors of the people, was to probe the whole Mosaic system until they reached the bedrock of cause and effect on which it rested. But this is just what they did not do. Their reverence for names was greater than their reverence for Truth and, assuming that Moses taught what he never did, they put to death the teacher of whom Moses had prophesied as the one who should complete his word in building up "the people of the I AM".

Thus they rejected "the Stone of Israel", and in so doing they fought against God --- that is, against the Law of Spirit in Self-evolution. For it was this Law, and this only, that the Carpenter of Nazareth taught. He came not to destroy the teachings of Moses and of the Prophets, but to fulfill them by showing what, under various veils and coverings, had been handed down through the generations. It was his mission to complete the Building of the Temple by exhibiting Perfected Man as the apex of the Pyramid of Evolution with himself being the first begotten of many brothers.

## The Evolutionary Pyramid

Broad and strong and deep was laid the foundation of this Pyramid in that first movement of the ONE which the Bible tells of in its opening words; and thenceforward the building has progressed through countless ages till Man, now sufficiently developed intellectually, requires only the final step of recognizing that the Universal Spirit reaches, in him, the reproduction of Itself in individuality to take his proper place as the crown and completion of the whole evolutionary process. He has to realize that the opening statement of Scripture concerning himself is not a mere figure of speech but a practical fact, and that he really is the image and likeness of the Universal Spirit.

This was the teaching of Jesus. When the Jews sought to stone him for saying that God was his Father (John 10:31), he replied by quoting the 82nd Psalm, "I said ye are gods", and laid stress on this as "Scripture that cannot be broken" --- in other words he stressed, "It is written in the very nature of things, by which each thing has its proper place in the universal order". He replied in effect, "I am only saying of myself what your own Law says of every one of you. I do not set myself forth as an exception, but as the example of what the nature of every man truly is". The same mistake has been perpetuated to the present day; but gradually people are beginning to see what the great truth is which Jesus taught and which Moses and the Prophets and the Psalms had proclaimed before him.

Perfected Man is the apex of the Evolutionary Pyramid, and this by a necessary sequence. First comes the Mineral Kingdom, lying inert and motionless, without any sort of individual recognition. Then comes the Vegetable Kingdom, capable of assimilating food, with individual life, but with only the most rudimentary intelligence, and rooted to one spot. Next comes the Animal Kingdom, where intelligence is manifestly on the increase, and the individual is no longer rooted to a single spot physically, yet is so intellectually, for its round of ideas is limited only to the supply of its bodily wants. Then comes the fourth or Human kingdom, where the individual is not rooted to one spot either physically or intellectually, for his thought can penetrate all space. But even he has not yet reached Liberty, for he is still the slave of "circumstances over which he has no control": his thoughts are unlimited, but they remain mere dreams until he can attain the power of giving them realization. Unlimited power of conception is his, but to complete his evolution he must acquire a corresponding power of creation. With that he will arrive at perfect Liberty.

Throughout the Four Kingdoms which have been developed, the progress from the lower to the higher is always towards greater liberty and therefore, in accordance with that principle of Continuity which Science recognizes as nowhere broken in Nature, Perfect Liberty must be the goal towards which the evolutionary process is tending. One state more is necessary to complete the Pyramid of Manifested nature: the addition of a Fifth Kingdom, which shall complete the work for which the four lower Kingdoms are the preparation --- the Kingdom in which Spirit shall be the ruling factor, and thus the Kingdom of Spirit which is the Kingdom of God.

## Mistaken Limitation

The uncertain mixed conditions among which we now live very accurately represent our uncertain and mixed modes of Thought. We think from the standpoint of a mixture of good and evil and have no certainty as to which is really the controlling power. Good, we say, works "within certain limits"; but who or what fixes those limits we cannot guess. In short, if we analyze the average belief of mankind as represented in Christian countries at the present day, it resolves itself into belief in a sort of rough-

and-tumble between God and Devil, in which sometimes one is uppermost and sometimes the other; and so we entirely lose the conception of a definite control by the Power of Good steadily acting in accordance with its own character and not subject to the dictation of some Evil Power which prescribes "certain limits" for it.

This balance between good and evil is undoubtedly the present state of things, but it is the reflection of our own Thought, and the remedy for it is therefore that knowledge of the inner Law which shows us that we ourselves are producing the evils we deplore. They all proceed from a denial of the Creative Power of our Thought --- in other words, the denial that Man is the "image of God". They proceed from the hypothesis that good can exist only "within certain limits", and that therefore our work must not be directed towards the producing of more good, but to scrambling for a larger share of the limited quantity of good that has been doled out to the world by a bankrupt Deity.

Whether this scramble be between individuals in the commercial world, or between classes in social life, or between nations in the glorious name of murder with the best modern weapons, the underlying principle is always that of competition based on the idea that the gain of one can only accrue by another's loss; and therefore what prevents us to-day from "entering into rest" (Psalm 95:11; Heb. 4:3) is the same cause that produced the same effect in the time of the Psalmist: "they could not enter in because of unbelief" and "they limited the Holy ONE of Israel". *So long as we persist in the belief that the truly originating causes of things are to be found anywhere but in our own mental attitude, we condemn ourselves to interminable toil and strife.*

## The Creative Power in Man

But if, instead of looking at conditions, we endeavored to realize First Cause as that which acts independently of all conditions, because the conditions flow from it and not vice versa, we should see that the whole teaching of the Bible is to lead us to understand that, because man is the image of God, he can never divest his Thought of its inherent creative power; and for this reason it sets before us the limitless goodness of the Heavenly Father as the model which in our own use of this power we are to follow. "He maketh His sun to rise on the evil and on the good, and sendeth his rain on the just and on the unjust" (Matt. 5:45). In other words, the Universal First Cause is not concerned with pre-existing conditions but continually radiates forth its creative energy, transmuting the evil into the good and the good into something still better; and since it is the prerogative of Man to use the same creative power from the standpoint of the individual, he must use it in the same manner if he would produce effects of Life and not of Death.

He cannot divest his Thought of its creative power, but it rests with him to choose between Life and Death according to the way in which he employs it. As each one realizes that conditions are created from within and not from without, he begins to see the force of the Master's invitation: "Come unto me all ye that labor and are heavy laden, and I will give you rest" (Matt. 11:28). He sees that the only thing that has prevented him from entering into rest has been unbelief in the limitless power of drawing from that inexhaustible storehouse; and when we thus realize the true nature of the Divine Law of Supply, we see that it depends not on taking from others without giving a fair equivalent, but rather on giving good measure pressed down and shaken together (Luke 6:38) [a Biblical expression of abundance, originally referring to grain].

The Creative Law is that the quality of the Thought which starts any particular chain of cause and effect continues through every link of the chain, and therefore if the originating Thought be that of the absolute goodness-in-itself of the intended creation, irrespective of all circumstances, then this quality will be inherent not only in the thing immediately created, but also in the whole incalculable series of results flowing from it.

Therefore, to make our work good for its own sake is the surest way to make it return to us in a rich harvest, which it will do by a natural Law of Growth if we only allow it time to grow. By degrees, each one of us finds this out for himself, and the eventual recognition of these truths by the mass of mankind must make "the desert rejoice and blossom as the rose" (Isaiah 35:1). Let each one therefore take part joyfully in the Building of the Temple, in which shall be offered, forever, the twofold worship of Glory to God and Goodwill to Man.

## Chapter 7
## THE SACRED NAME

### What's In a Name?

A point that can hardly fail to strike the Bible student is the frequency with which we are directed to the Name of the Lord as the source of strength and protection instead of to God Himself; and the steady uniformity of this practice, both in the Old and New Testaments, clearly indicates the intention to put us upon some special line of inquiry with regard to the Sacred Name. Not only is this suggested by the frequency of the expression, but the Bible gives a very remarkable instance which shows that the Sacred Name must be considered as a formula containing a summary of all wisdom.

The Master tells us that the Queen of the South came to hear the wisdom of Solomon, and if we turn to 1 Kings 10:1, we find that the fame of Solomon's wisdom, which induced the Queen of Sheba to come to prove him with hard questions, was "concerning the *Name* of the Lord". This accords with the immemorial tradition of the Jews, that the knowledge of the secret Name of God enables him who possesses it to perform the most stupendous miracles.

This Hidden Name was revealed, they say, to Moses and taught by him to Aaron and handed on by him to his successors. It was the secret enshrined in the Holy of Holies and was scrupulously guarded by the successive High Priests. It is the supreme secret, and its knowledge is the supreme object of attainment. Thus tradition and Scripture alike point to "The NAME" as the source of Light and Life, and Deliverance from all evil.

May we not therefore suppose that this must be the veiled statement of some great Truth? The purpose of a name is to call up, by a single word, the complete idea of the thing named, with all those qualities and relations that make it what it is, instead of having to describe all this in detail every time we want to suggest the conception of it. The correct name of a thing thus conveys the idea of its whole nature, and accordingly the correct Name of God should, in some manner, be a concise statement of the Divine Nature as the Source of all Life, Wisdom, Power, and Goodness, and the Origin of all manifested being.

For this reason the Bible puts before us "the Name of the Lord" not only as the object of supreme reverence, but also as the grand subject of study, by means of which we may command the Power that will provide us with all good and protect us from all ill. Let us, then, see what we can learn regarding this marvelous Name.

### ONE-ness

The Bible calls the Divine Being by a variety of Names, but when we have once got the general clue to the Sacred name, we shall find that each of them implies all the others, since each suggests some particular aspect of **THAT** which is the All-embracing **UNIT**, the everlasting **ONE**, which cannot be divided, and any one aspect of which must therefore convey to the instructed mind the suggestion of all the others. We will therefore seek first this general clue which will throw light on more particular applications.

### "The Sacred Name" is "The Lost Word"

Much search has been made by many for "the Lost Word", that "Word of Power" the possession of which makes all things possible to him who discovers it. Great students of bygone days devoted their lives to this search, and, so far as the outside world judges, without any result, but now the tide is beginning to turn, and improved methods of scientific research are approaching from the physical side, that One Great Centrex in which all lines of truth eventually converge; and so the fast-spreading recognition of Man's spiritual nature is leading once more to the search for "the Word of Power". And rightly did the old Hebrew builders and their followers in the fifteenth, sixteenth, and seventeenth centuries connect this "Lost Word" with the Sacred name; but whether because they purposely surrounded it with mystery, or because the simplicity of the truth proved a stumbling-block to them, their open writings only indicate a search through endless mazes, while the clue to the labyrinth lay in the Word itself.

Are we any nearer its discovery now? The answer is at once Yes and No. The "Lost Word" was as close to those old thinkers as it is to us, but to those whose eyes and ears are sealed by prejudice, it will always remain as far off as though it belonged to another planet. It is concealed from the seekers only by its very conspicuousness. The concealment of the "Lost Word" lies in its absolute simplicity.

Nothing so commonplace could possibly be it, and yet the Scripture plainly tells us that its intimate familiarity is the token by which we shall know it. We need not say, "Who shall go up for us to heaven and bring it unto us, that we may hear it and do it? Neither is it beyond the sea that thou shouldst say, Who shall go over the sea for us and bring it unto us, that we hear it and do it? But the Word is very nigh unto thee, in thy mouth and in thy heart, that thou mayest do it" (Deut. 30: 12-14). Realize that the only "Word of Power" is the Divine Name, and the mystery at once flashes into light.

The "Lost Word" which we have been seeking to discover with pain and cost and infinite study has been all the time in our heart and in our mouth. It is nothing else than that familiar expression which we use so many times a day: *I AM*. This is the Divine

Name revealed to Moses at the burning bush, and if we believe that the Bible means what it says when it tells us that Man is the image and likeness of God, then we shall see that the same statement of Being, which in the Universal applies to God, must in the individual and particular apply to Man also.

This "Word" is always in our hearts, for the consciousness of our own individuality consists only in the recognition that *I AM*, and the assertion of our own being, as one of the necessities of ordinary speech is upon our lips continually. Thus the "Word of Power" is close at hand to everyone, and it continues to be the "Lost Word" only because of our ignorance of all that is enfolded in it.

## Teachings of Moses and Jesus

A comparison of the teaching of Moses and Jesus will show that they are two complementary statements of the one fundamental truth of the "*I AM*". Moses views this truth from the standpoint of Universal being and sees man evolving from the Infinite Mind and subject to it as the Great Law-giver. Jesus views it from the standpoint of the individual and sees Man comprehending the Infinite by limitless expansion of his own mind, and thus returning to the Universal Mind as a son coming back to his natural place in the house of his father.

Each is necessary to the correct understanding of the other, and thus Jesus came not to abolish the work of Moses, but to complete it. *The "I AM" is ever in the forefront of his teaching: "I AM the Way, the Truth, and the Life" [John 14:6]; "I AM the Resurrection and the Life" [John 11:25]; "Except ye believe I AM ye shall perish in your sins" [John 8:24].* **These and similar sayings shine forth with marvelous radiance when once we see that he was not speaking of himself personally, but of the**

*Individualized Principle of Being in the generic sense which is applicable to all mankind.*

**What is wanted is our recognition of that innermost self which is pure Spirit**, *and therefore not subject to any conditions whatever, in fact all conditions are made by it, and the first two conditions made by it are Time and Space; and since these two primary conditions can have no place in essential being and are only created by its Thought, the true recognition of the "I AM" is a recognition of the Self, which sees Time and Space as eternally subsisting in its own Being, sending forth all forms at its will and withdrawing them again as needed.*

*To know this is to know Life-in-itself; and any knowledge short of this is only to know the appearance of Life, to recognize merely the activity of the vehicles through which it functions, while failing to recognize the motive power itself. It is recognizing only "the individual" without "the Universal". The "Word of Power" which sets us free is the* whole *Divine Name, and not one part of it without the other. It is the separation of its two portions that has caused the long and weary pilgrimage of mankind through the ages.*

The separation of the two elements of the Divine Name is not true in the Heart of Being, but Man, by reasoning only from the testimony of the outward senses, forcibly puts asunder what God forever joins together; and it is because the Bridegroom has thus been taken away that the children of the bride-chamber have been starved and lack richness when they ought to have feasted with continual joy.

But the Great Marriage of Heaven and Earth at last takes place, and all nature joins in the song of exultation, whose cadences roll on through the ages, ever spreading into fresh harmonies as new themes evolve from the first grand wedding march which celebrates the eternal union of the Mystical Marriage.

When this union is realized by the individual as subsisting in himself, then the *I AM* becomes to him personally all that the Master said it would. He realizes that it is in him a deathless principle and that though its mode of self-expression may alter, its essential Being-ness, which is the *I Myself* consciousness in each of us, never can; and so this principle is found to be in us both Life and Resurrection. As Life, it never ceases; and as Resurrection, it is continually providing higher and higher forms for its expression of *Itself*, which is ourself.

No matter what may be our particular theory of the specific method of operation by which this renewal takes place, there can be no mistake about the principle; our physical theory of the Resurrection may be wrong, but the Law that Life will always provide a suitable form, for its self-expression is unchangeable and universal and must, therefore, be as true of the Life-Principle manifesting itself as the individuality which *I AM*, as in all its other modes of manifestation.

When we thus realize the true nature of the *I AM* that *I AM* --- that is, the Being-ness that I Myself AM --- we discover that the *whole* principle of Being is in ourselves --- not "the individual" only, but "the Universal" also; and this being the case, we no longer have to go with our pitcher to draw our water from a well outside, for now we discover that the exhaustless spring of Living Water is within ourselves.

Now we can see why it is that except we believe in the *I AM*, we must perish in our sins, for "sin is the transgression of the Law" [1 John 3:4], and ignorant infraction of the Law will bring its penalty as certainly as willful infraction. "Ignorance of the law is no excuse" is a legal maxim which is seen throughout Nature, and the innocent child who ignorantly applies a lit match to a barrel of gunpowder will be as ruthlessly blown up as the mobster who perishes in the perpetration of some hideous crime. If, therefore, we ignorantly controvert the Law of our own Being, we must suffer the inevitable consequences by our failure to rise into that Life of Liberty and Joy which the full knowledge of the power of our *I AM*-ness must necessarily carry with it.

## Liberty

Let us remember that Perfect Liberty is our goal.

The perfect Law is the Law of Liberty. The Tree of Life is the Tree of Liberty, and it is not a plant of spontaneous growth; but as the center of the Mystical Garden, it is its chief glory and therefore deserves the most diligent cultivation. But it yields its produce as it grows and does not keep us waiting till it reaches maturity before giving us any reward for work; for if maturity means a point at which it will grow no more, then it will never reach maturity, for since the ground in which this Tree has its root is the Eternal Life-in-itself, there is nowhere in the Universe any power to limit its growth and so, under intelligent cultivation, it will go on expanding into increasing strength, beauty, and fruitfulness forever.

This is the meaning of the Scriptural saying, "His reward is with him and his work before him" (Isaiah 40:10 and 62:11). Ordinarily, we should suppose it would be the other way; but when we see that the possibilities of self-expansion are endless and depend on our intelligent study and work, and that at every step of the way we are bound to derive all present benefit from the degree of knowledge we are working up to, it becomes clear that the Bible, rightly interpreted, has kept the right order, and that always our reward is *with* us and our work *before* us; for the reward is the continually increasing joy and glory of perpetually unfolding Life.

All along the line our progress depends on working up to the knowledge we possess, for what we do not act up to we do not really believe; and the power which will overcome all difficulties is confidence in the Eternal "Life-in-ourself", which is the individualized expression of the *"ONE I AM"* that spoke to Moses at the burning bush.

## Three Aspects

We find, then, two aspects of the Sacred name: one which presents it as the Universal *I AM*, the All-productive Power which is the root of all manifestation, and the other indicative of the reciprocal relation between this Power and the individual soul. *But **there is yet a third aspect under which this Power may be viewed**, and **that is as working through the individual who has become conscious of his own relation to it and of his consequent direction and instruction by it***. In this sense the Old Testament enumerates its Names in the text: "His Name shall be called Wonderful, Counselor, the Mighty God, the Everlasting Father, and the Prince of Peace" (Isaiah 9:6). In the Book of Job this is called "the Interpreter" (3:23), and in the New Testament this Name is called "The Word".

## The Word

With these preliminary remarks, I would lay particular stress upon the Name given to the Universal Principle in its Third aspect, that of manifestation through the individual mind. In this sense it is emphatically called "The Word", and a study of comparative religions shows that this conception of the Universal Mind, manifesting Itself as Speech, has been reached by all the great race-religions in their deeper significances. The "*Logos*" of

Greek philosophy, the *"Vach"* of the Sanskrit, are typical instances, and the reason is to be found, as in all statements of truth, in the nature of the thing itself.

The Biblical account of creation represents the work as completed by the appearing of Man; that is to say, the evolutionary process culminates in the Creative Principle expressing Itself in a form differing from all lower ones in its capacity for reasoning. Now reasoning implies the use of words either spoken or employed mentally, for whether we wish to make the stages of an argument plain to another or to ourselves, it can only be done by putting the sequence of cause and effect into *words*.

The first idea suggested by the principle of Speech is, therefore, that of individual intelligence, and next, as following from this, we get the idea of expressing individual will; then, as we begin to realize the reciprocal relation between the Universal Mind and the individual mind, which necessarily results from the latter being an evolution from the former, our conception of intelligence and volition becomes extended from the individual to the Universal, and we see that because these qualities exist in human personality, they must exist *in some more generalized mode* in that Universal Mind, of which the individual mind is a more specialized reproduction; and so we arrive at the result that the Speech-principle is the highest expression of the Divine Wisdom, Power, and Love, whose combined action produces what we call Creation.

In this sense, then, the Bible attributes the creation of the world to the Divine Word, and it therefore rightly says that "In the beginning was The Word, and The Word was with God, and The Word was God", and that without The Word "was not anything made that was made"; and from this commencement, the natural sequence of evolution brings us to the crowning result in the manifestation of The Word as Man, at first ignorant of his Divine origin, but nevertheless containing all the potentialities which the recognition of his true nature as the image of God will enable him to develop. And when at length this recognition comes to anyone, he arises and returns to "The Father", and in the discovery of his true relation to the Divine Mind finds that he also is a child of the Almighty and can speak "the Word of Power".

He may have been the prodigal who has wasted his substance, or the respectable brother who thought that only limited supplies were doled out to him; but as soon as the truth dawns upon him, he realizes the meaning of the words, "Son, thou art always with Me, and all that I have is thine" [Luke 15:31].

In Its Third aspect as "the Word", the Universal Principle becomes specialized. In its earlier modes it is the Life-Principle working by a Law of Averages, and thus maintaining the race as a whole, but not providing special accommodation for the individual. And it is inconceivable that the Cosmic Power, as such, should ever pass beyond what we may call the administration of the world in a global sense, for to suppose It doing so would involve the self-contradiction of the Universal acting on the plane of the Particular without becoming the particular; and it is precisely by *becoming* the particular, or by evolution into individual minds, that it carries on the work beyond the stage at which things are governed by a mere Law of Averages.

It is thus that we become "fellow-workers with God" and that "the Father" is represented as inviting His sons to work in His vineyard. By recognition of his own true place in the scheme of evolution, Man learns that his function is to *carry on* the work which has been begun in the Universal to still further applications in the Particular, thus affording the key to the Master's words, "My Father worketh *hitherto, and* I work" [John 5:17]; and the instrument by which the instructed man does this is his knowledge of the Sacred Name in its Threefold significance.

The study of the sacred name is the study of the Livingness of Being and of the Law of Expression in all its phases, and no book or library of books is sufficient to cope with such a vast idea. All any writer can do is to point out the broad lines of the subject, and each reader must make his own personal application of it. But the Law remains forever, that the sincere desire for Truth produces a corresponding unfoldment of Truth, and ***the supreme Truth is reached in that final recognition of the Divine Name.***

## Chapter 8
## THE DEVIL

### Opposites

It is impossible to read the Bible and ignore the important part which it assigns to the Devil. The Devil first appears as the Serpent in the story of "the Fall" and figures throughout Scripture till the final scene in Revelation, where "the old Serpent, which is the Devil and Satan", is cast into the lake of fire. What, then, is meant by the Devil? We may start with the self-obvious proposition that "God" and the "Devil" must be the exact opposites of each other. Whatever God is, the Devil is not. Since God is Being, the Devil is Not-Being. And so we are met by the paradox that though the Bible says so much about the Devil, yet the Devil does not exist. It is precisely this fact of non-existence that makes up the Devil; it is that power which in appearance is, and in reality is not; in a word, it is the Suggestion of the Negative.

We are put upon this track by the statement in 2 Corinthians 1:20 that in Christ, all the promises of God are Yea and Amen --- that is, *essentially Affirmative*; in other words, that all our growth towards Perfected Humanity must be by recognition of the Positive and not by recognition of the Negative. The prime fact of Negation is its Nothingness, but, owing to the impossibility of ever divesting our Thought of its Creative Power, our *conception* of the Negative as something having a substantive existence of its own gives it a very real power indeed, and it is this power that the Bible calls "the Devil and Satan", the same old Serpent which we find beguiling Eve in the Book of Genesis. It is equally a mistake to say that there is an Evil Power or that there is not. Let us examine this paradox.

## Only One Good

A little consideration will show us unless the Infinite and Universal Power were Creative, nothing could exist. If it be creative, then it is the Life-Principle working always for self-expression, and to suppose the undifferentiated principle of Life acting otherwise than life-givingly would contradict the very idea of its livingness.

Whatever tends to expand and improve life is the Good, and therefore, it is a primary intuition from which we cannot get away, that the Infinite, Originating, and Maintaining Power can only be Good. But to find this absolute and unchangeable "Good", we are required to get to the very bedrock of Being, to that as yet undifferentiated Life-in-itself inherent in, and forming one with, Universal Primordial Substance, of which I have spoken in a former chapter [see - page 78]. This All-underlying Life is forever expressing itself through Form; but the Form is not the Life, and it is from not seeing this that so much confusion arises.

The Universal Life-Principle, simply as such, finds expression as much in one form as another, and is just as active in the scattered particles before it makes a human body as it is in those particles when they cohered together in the living man; this is merely the well-recognized scientific truth of the Conservation of Energy.

## Life Power Higher Than Atomic Power

On the other hand, we cannot help perceiving that there is something in the individual which exercises a greater power than the perpetual energy residing in the ultimate atoms; for otherwise what is it that maintains in our bodies for perhaps a century the unstable equilibrium of atomic forces which, when that something is withdrawn, cannot continue for twenty-four hours?

Is this something another something than that which is at work as the perpetual energy within the atoms? No, for otherwise there would be two originating powers in the Universe, and if our study of the Bible teaches us anything, it is that the Originating Power is only ***ONE***; and we must therefore conceive of the Power we are examining as the same Power that resides in the ultimate atoms, only now working at a higher level. It has welded the atoms into a distinct organism, and so, to distinguish this mode of power from the mere atomic energies, we may call it the Integrating Power, or the Power that Builds Up.

Now evolution is a continuous process of building up of more and more complex organisms, culminating at last in the production of Man as an organism both physically and mentally capable of expressing the Life of the Supreme Intelligence by means of the Individual Consciousness. Why, then, should not the Power, which is able to carry on the race as a perpetually improving expression of itself, do the same thing *in the individual*? That is the question with which we have to deal; in other words, why need the individual die? Why should he not go on in a perpetual expansion?

## Mortality

This question may seem absurd in the light of past experience. Those who believe only in blind forces answer that death is the law of Nature, and those who believe in the Divine Wisdom answer that it is the appointment of God. But strange as it may seem, both these answers are wrong. That death should be the ultimate law of Nature contradicts the principle of continuity as exemplified in the Lifeward tendency of evolution; and that it is the will of God is most emphatically denied by the Bible, for it tells us that he that has the power of death is the Devil (Hebrews 2:14). There is no beating about the bush; not God but the Devil sends death. There is no getting out of these plain words. So now let us examine this statement.

We have seen that whatever God is, the devil must be the opposite, and therefore if God is the Power that builds up, the Integrating power, the devil must be the power that pulls down, or the disintegrating power. Now what is disintegration? It is the breaking down of what was previously "a perfect whole". But what is it that causes the breaking down? It is still the Building-up Power, only the Law of Affinity by which it works is now acting from an inverted idea.

## Diversion And Distraction

The Universal Power is still at its building work, only it seems to have lost sight of its original motive and to have taken up fresh motives in other directions. And this is precisely the state of the case; it is just the want of continuous motive that causes disintegration. The only possible motive of the All-originating Life-Principle must be the expression of Life, and therefore we may picture it as continually seeking to embody itself in intelligences which are able to grasp its motive and co-operate with it by keeping that motive constantly in mind.

Granted that this *individualization of motive* could take place, there appears no reason why it should not continue to work on indefinitely. A tree is an organized center of life, but without the intelligence which would enable it to individualize the motive of the Universal Life-Principle. It individualizes a certain measure of the Universal Vital Energy, but it does not individualize the Universal Intelligence, and therefore when the measure of energy which it has individualized is exhausted, it dies; and the same thing happens with animals and men.

But as the particular intelligence advances in the recognition of itself as the individualization of the Universal Intelligence it becomes more and more capable of seizing upon the initial *motive* of the Universal Mind and giving it, and therefore itself, permanence. And supposing this recognition to be complete, the logical result would be never-ceasing and perpetually expanding individual life, thus bringing us back to those promises which I have quoted in the opening pages of this book, and reminding us of the Master's statement to the woman of Samaria that "the Father" is always "seeking" those who will worship Him in spirit and in truth; that is, those who can enter into the spirit, the motive, of what "the Father" is aiming at.

But what happens in the absence of a perfect recognition of the Universal Motive is that sooner or later the machinery runs down, and the "motive" is transferred to other centers where the same process is repeated, and so Life and Death alternate with each other in a ceaseless round. The disintegrating process is the Universal Builder taking the materials for fresh constructions from a tenement without a tenant; that is, from an organism which has not reached the measure of intelligence necessary to perpetuate the Universal Motive in itself or, as the Master put it in the parable of the ten virgins, such as have not a supply of oil to keep their lamps burning [Matt. 25].

This Negative disintegrating force is the Integrating Power working, so to say, at a lower level relatively to that at which it had been working in the organism that is being dissolved. It is not another power. Both the Bible, rightly interpreted, and common sense tell us that ultimately there can be only **ONE** power in the Universe which must, therefore, be the Building-power, so that there can be no such thing as a power which is negative in *itself*; but it shows itself negatively in *relation to the particular individual*, if through want of recognition he fails to provide the requisite conditions for it to work positively.

It will always continue to work for its very being is ceaseless activity; but whether it will act positively or negatively towards any particular individual depends entirely on whether he provides positive or negative conditions for its manifestation.

We see, then, that what gives the Positive Power a negative action is the failure to intelligently recognize our own individualization of it. In the lower forms of life this failure is inevitable, because they are not provided with an organism capable of such a recognition. In Man, the suitable organism is present, but he seeks knowledge only from past experiences which have necessarily been of the negative order, and does not, by the combined action of reason and faith, look into the Infinite for the unfoldment of limitless possibilities; and so he employs his intelligence to deny that which, if he affirmed it, would be in him the spring of perpetual renovation.

## Denial of the Affirmative

The Power of the Negative, therefore, has its root in the denial of the Affirmative; and so we die because we have not yet learned to understand the Principle of Life; we have yet to learn the great Law, that "the higher mode of intelligence controls the lower". In consequence of our ignorance, we attribute an affirmative power to the Negative --- that is to say, the power of taking an initiative on its own account, not seeing that it is a *condition* resulting from the absence of something more positive; and so the power of the Negative consists in affirming that to be true which is not true, and for this reason it is called in scripture the father of lies, or that principle from which all false statements are generated.

The word "Devil" means "false accuser" or "false affirmer", and this name is therefore in itself sufficient to show us that what is meant is the creative principle of Affirmation used in the wrong direction, a truth which has been handed down to us from the

Ancients in the saying "The Devil is God inverted". This is how it is that "the Devil" can be a vast impersonal power while at the same time having no existence, and so the paradox with which we started is solved. And now it becomes clear why we are told that "the Devil" has the power of death. It is not held by a personal individual, but results quite naturally from that ignorant and inverted Thought which is "the Spirit that denies".

This is the exact opposite to "the Son of God", in whom all things are only "Yea and Amen". That is the Spirit of the Affirmative and, therefore, the Spirit of Life; and so it is that the Son of God was manifested that "he might destroy him that had the power of death, that is, the Devil, and deliver them who, through fear of death, were all in their lifetime subject to bondage" (Hebrews 2:14-15).

## Satan

Again, we are told that the Devil is Satan.

Now, taken in due order, Matter or Concrete Form is as necessary as Spirit itself, for without it there could be no manifestation of Spirit; in other words, there could be no existence at all. Seen from this point of view, there is nothing evil in it, but on the contrary, it may be compared to the lamp which concentrates the light and gives it a particular direction, and in this respects Matter is called "*Lucifer*" or the Light-bearer. This is Matter taking its proper place in the order of the Kingdom of Heaven. But if "*Lucifer*" falls from Heaven, becomes rebellious, and endeavors to usurp the place of *"The Life Giving Principle"*, then it is the fallen Archangel and becomes "*Satan*".

Thus "Satan" is the same old Serpent that deceived Eve; it is the wrong belief that sets merely secondary causes, which are only conditions, in the place of First Cause or that originating power of Thought which makes enlightened Man the image of his Maker and the Son of God. [For the all-important distinction between Causes and Conditions, see Chapter 15 of *"The Essential THOMAS TROWARD"*.]

## The Antidote

We thus see that the whole question of the power of evil turns on the two fundamental Laws which I spoke of in the opening pages of this book as forming the basis of Bible teaching: the Law of Suggestion and the Law of the Creative Power of Thought. The conception of an abstract principle of evil, the Devil, receives its power from our own autosuggestion of its existence; and the power of evil results from a mental attitude which allows us to receive these suggestions.

Then in both cases, the suggestion having been accepted, our own creative power of Thought does the rest and so prepares the way for receiving still further suggestions of the same sort. Now the antidote to all this is a right conception of God or the Universal Spirit of Life as the ***ONE*** and only originating Power. If we realize that relatively to us this Power manifests itself through the medium of our own Thought, and that in so doing it in no way changes its inherent quality of Life-givingness, this recognition will constitute such a supremely powerful and all-embracing Suggestion as must necessarily eradicate all suggestions of a contrary description; and so our Thought, being based on this Supreme Suggestion of Good, is certain to have a correspondingly life-giving character.

To recognize the essential One-ness of this Power is to recognize it as God, and to recognize its essential Life-givingness is to recognize it as Love, and so we shall realize in ourselves the truth that "God is Love". Then "if God be for us, who can be against us?" (Romans 8:31) and so we realize the further truth that "perfect love casteth out fear" (1 John 4:18), with the result that in our own world there can be no devil.

## Chapter 9
## THE LAW OF LIBERTY

### The Old And The New

Nothing is more indicative of our ignorance regarding the purpose and meaning of the Bible than when we seek to draw a distinction between the Law and the Gospel. This is foolishness. The Gospel doesn't try to change the Law one wit. The Law which the Bible sets forth from first to last is the Law of Human Individuality. The Bible rightfully interpreted is the Spiritual Natural History Book of Man. It begins with his creation by evolution from the kingdoms which had preceded him, and it terminates with his elevation to Divine status. The line is long, but it is straight, and reaches its glorious destination by an orderly sequence of cause and effect. It is the statement of the evolution of the individual as the result of his recognition of the Law by which he came to be a human being at all. When he sees that this happened neither by chance nor by arbitrary command, then, and not till then, will he wake up to the fact that he is what he is by reason of a Law inherent in himself, the action of which he can therefore carry on indefinitely by correctly understanding and cheerfully following it.

### Liberty According to Law

His first general perception that there is such a Law at all is followed by the realization that it must be the Law of his own individuality, for he has only discovered the existence of the Law by recognizing himself as the Expression of it; and therefore he finds that, before all else, the Law is that he shall be himself. But a Law which allows us to be ourselves is Perfect Liberty, and thus we get back to St James' statement that the Perfect Law is the Law of Liberty.

Obviously it is not Liberty, as some religions claim, to allow ourselves to be depressed into such a mental attitude of submission to every form and degree of misery as coming to us "by the will of God" that we at last reach a condition of apathy in which one blow more or less makes very little difference. Such teaching is based on the Devil's beatitude --- "Blessed are they that expect nothing, for they shall not be disappointed" --- but that is not the Gospel of Deliverance which Jesus preached in his first discourse in the synagogue of Nazareth. Jesus' teaching was not the deification of suffering, but the fullness of Joy; and he emphatically declared that all bondage --- everything which keeps us from enjoying our life to the full --- is the working of that Power of the Negative which the Bible calls the Devil. To give up hope and regard ourselves as the sport of an inexorable fate is not Liberty. It is not obedience to a higher power, but abject submission to a lower --- the power of ignorance, unintelligence, and negation.

### Harmony or Disturbance???

*Perfect Liberty is the consciousness that we are not thus bound by any power of evil but that, on the contrary, we are centers in which the Creative Spirit of the Universe finds particular expression.* Then we are in harmony with its continual progressive movement towards still more perfect modes of expression, and therefore its thought and our thought, its action and our action, become identical, so that in expressing the Spirit we express ourselves. When we reach this unity of consciousness, we cannot but find it to be perfect Liberty; for our own self-expression, being also that of the All-creating Spirit as it manifests in our individuality, is no longer bound by prior conditions, but starts afresh from the standpoint of Original Creative Energy.

This is Liberty according to Law, the Law of the All-creating Harmony, in which God's way and our way coincide. The idea of Liberty, without a unifying Harmony as its basis, is inconceivable, for with everyone struggling to get their own way at *somebody else's expense*, you create a disturbance, and that is just why there is so much of that element in the world at the present time. But such an inverted idea of liberty is based on the assumption that Man does not possess the power of controlling his conditions by his Thought; in other words, the flat denial of the initial statement of Scripture regarding him that he is made "in the image and likeness of God".

Once grant the creative power of our Thought and there is an end of struggling for our own way, and an end of gaining it at *someone else's expense*; for, since by the terms of the hypothesis we can create what we like through our own thought, the simplest way of getting what we want is not to snatch it from somebody else, but to make it for ourselves; and since there is no limit to Thought, there can be no need for straining; and for everyone to have his own way in *this* manner would be to banish all strife, want, sickness, and sorrow from the earth.

### Faith in God

Now it is precisely on this assumption of the creative power of our Thought that the whole Bible rests. If not, what is the meaning of being saved by Faith? Faith is essentially Thought; and therefore every call to have Faith in God is a call to trust in the power of our own Thought about God. "According to your faith be it unto you" [Matt. 15:28], says the New Testament. "As a man thinketh in his heart, so is he" [Prov. 23:7], says the Old Testament. The entire Book is nothing but one continuous statement of the Creative Power of Thought.

The whole Bible is a commentary on the text, "Man is the image and likeness of God". And it comments on this text sometimes by explaining why, by reason of the ***ONE***-ness of the Spirit, this must necessarily be so; sometimes by incitements to emotional states calculated to call this power into activity; sometimes by precepts warning us against those emotions which would produce its inverse action; sometimes by the example of those who have successfully demonstrated this power, and conversely by examples of those who have perverted it; sometimes by statements of the terrible consequences that must inevitably follow such perversion; and sometimes by glorious promises of the illimitable possibilities residing in this wonderful power if used in the right way; and thus it is that "All Scripture is profitable for doctrine, for reproof, for correction, for instruction in righteousness" (2 Tim. 3:16).

All this proceeds from the initial assumption with which the Bible starts regarding ***man***, that he ***is the reproduction in individuality of that which God is in Universality***. Start with this assumption, and the whole Bible works out logically. Deny it, and the Book becomes nothing but a mass of inconsistencies and contradictions. The value of the Bible as a storehouse of knowledge and a guide into Life depends entirely on our attitude with regard to its fundamental proposition.

But this proposition contains in itself the Affirmation of our Liberty; and the Gospel preached by Jesus amounts simply to this, that if anyone realizes himself as the reproduction, in conscious individuality, of the same principles which the Law of the Old Testament bids us recognize in the Divine Mind, he will thereby enter upon an unlimited inheritance of Life and Liberty. But to do this we must realize the Divine image in ourselves on *all lines*.

## Consistency

We cannot enter upon a full life of Joy and Liberty by trying to realize the Divine image along one line only. If we seek to reproduce the Creative Power without its correlatives of Wisdom and Love, we shall do so only to our own injury; for there is one thing which is impossible alike to God and man, and that is to plant a seed of one sort and make it yield fruit of another. We can never get beyond the Law that the effect must be of the same nature as the cause. To abrogate this Law would be to destroy the very foundation of the Creative Power of Thought, for then we could never reckon upon what our Thought might produce; so that the very same Law which places creative power at our disposal necessarily provides punishment for its misuse and reward for its right employment.

And this is equally the case along the two other lines. To seek development only on the line of Knowledge is to contemplate a store of wealth while remaining ignorant of the one fact which gives it any value: that it is our *own*; and, in like manner, to cultivate only Love makes our great motive power evaporate in a weak sentimentality which accomplishes nothing, because it does not know *how* and does not feel *able*. So here we see the force of the Master's words when he bids us aim at a perfection like that of our "Father" in heaven, a perfection based on the knowledge that all being is threefold in essence and one in expression; and that therefore we can attain Liberty only by recognizing this universal Law in ourselves also; and that, accordingly, the Thought that sets us free must be a simultaneous movement along all three lines of our nature.

The Divine Mind may be represented by a large circle and the individual mind by a small one, but that is no reason why the smaller circle should not be as perfect for its own area as the larger; and therefore the initial statement of the Bible that Man is the image of God is the charter of Individual Liberty for each one, provided we realize that this likeness must extend to the whole threefold unity that is ourself, and not to a part only. Our Liberty, therefore, consists in being ourselves in our Wholeness, and this means the conscious exercise of all our powers, whether of our visible or invisible personality. It means being ourselves, not trying to be somebody else.

## Universal Principles

The *principles* by which anyone ever attains to self-expression, whether in the humblest or the most exalted degree, are always the same, for they are Universals and apply to everyone alike, and therefore we may advantageously study their working in the lives of others; but to suppose that the expression of these principles is bound to take the same form in us that it did in the individual who is the object of our hero-worship, is to deny the first principle of manifested being, which is Individuality.

If someone towers above the crowd, it is because he has grown to that height, and I cannot permanently attain the same elevation by climbing on his shoulders but only by growing to the same height myself. Therefore, the attempt to copy a particular individual, however beautiful his character, is bondage and a relinquishing of our birthright of Selfhood.

What we have to do in studying those lives which we admire is to discover the Universal principles which those persons embodied in their way, and then set to work to embody them in ours. To do this is to realize the Universal *I AM* manifesting itself in every Individuality; and when we see this, we find that the statement of the Law of Individual Liberty is the declaration that was made to Moses at the burning bush and is the truth that Jesus proclaimed when he said that it was the recognition of the *I AM* that would set us free from the Law of bondage and death.

In speaking of the *I AM* as the Principle of Life, neither Jesus nor Moses used the words personally, and Jesus especially avoids any such misconstruction by saying, "If I bear witness of myself, my witness is not true" [John 5:31]; in other words, he came to set forth not himself personally, but those great principles common to all mankind, of which he exemplified the full development.

There is the whole secret, and when we come down --- or rather when we rise --- to the level of these souls whose pure intuitions have not been warped by arguments drawn only from the outside of things, we see that the principle of continual self-creation into all varieties of individuality affords the true clue to all that we are and to all that is around us; and when we see this, the teaching regarding the *I AM* in ourselves becomes clear, logical, and simple.

Then we understand that the Law of our Whole Being --- that which is Cause as well as Effect --- is the reproduction in Individuality of the same Power which makes the worlds; and when this is understood in its Wholeness, we see that this principle cannot, as manifested in us, be in opposition to its manifestation of itself in other forms. The Whole must be homogeneous; that which is homogeneous cannot act in opposition to itself; and consequently this homogeneous principle, which underlies all individuality and is the *I AM* in each, can never act contrary to the Law of Life. Therefore, to know ourselves as the concentration of this principle into a focus of self-recognition is to be at one with the Life-Principle which is in all worlds and under all forms.

## Natural Education

We may well transfer the whole description of conscious sufferings to that of the outer man, and the reason for these sufferings is the want of Wholeness; they are the result of trying to live only in one portion of our nature --- and that the lower --- instead of in the Whole, and consequently these sufferings will continue until we realize that an even balance of all parts of our nature is what constitutes true individuality, or that which is without division.

By the buffeting of experience, the lower personality is being continually driven to inquire more and more into the reason for its sufferings, and as it grows in intelligence, it sees that they always result from some willful or ignorant infraction of the Law of Things-as-they-are, as distinguished from Things-as-they-look; and so by degrees the lower personality grows into union with the higher personality of Things-as-they-are until at last the two are found to be ***ONE***, and the Perfected Man stands forth Whole.

This is the process to which the writer of the Epistle to the Hebrews refers when he says that "though he were a son, yet learned he obedience by the things which he suffered" [Heb. 5:8], thus indicating a course of education which can only apply to a personality whose evolution is not yet completed. But by these sufferings of the lower personality the salvation of the entire individuality is at length accomplished for, being thus led to study the Law of the Whole, the lower or simply intellectual mentality at last discovers its relation to the Intuitive and Creative Principle and realizes that nothing short of harmonious union of the two makes a Complete Man. Until this recognition takes place, the real meaning of suffering is not understood.

To talk about "the Mystery of Pain" is like talking about the mystery of broken glass if we throw a stone at a window --- it is of our own making. We attribute our sufferings to "the will of God" simply because we can think of nothing else to attribute them to, being ignorant alike of ourselves as centers of causation and of God as the Universal Life-Principle which cannot will evil against anyone. So long as we are at this stage of intelligence, we esteem the lower personality (the only self we yet know) to be "stricken and smitten of God" --- we put it all down to God's account --- while all the time the cause of our wounding and bruising was not the will of God, but our own infractions of the Law of causation or the want of even balance between all portions of our Individuality without which the liberating recognition of our own *I AM*-ness can never take place.

## A Gospel of Peace

The Law of Man's Individuality is therefore the Law of Liberty, and equally it is the Gospel of Peace; for when we truly understand the Law of our own individuality, we see that the same Law finds its expression in everyone else, and consequently we shall reverence the Law in others exactly in proportion as we value it in ourselves. To do this is to follow the Golden Rule of doing to others what we would they should do unto us; and because we know that the Law of Liberty in ourselves must include the free use of our own creative power, there is no longer any inducement to infringe the rights of others, for we can satisfy all our desires by the exercise of our knowledge of the Law.

As this comes to be understood, co-operation will take the place of competition with the result of removing all ground of enmity, whether between individuals, classes, or nations; and thus the continual recognition of the Divine or "highest" principles in ourselves brings "peace on earth and good-will among men" naturally in its train, and it is for this reason that the Bible everywhere couples the reign of peace on earth with the Knowledge of God.

The whole object of the Bible is to teach us to be ourselves and yet more ourselves. It does not trouble itself with political or social questions, or even with those of religious organization, but it goes to the root of all, which is the Individual. First set people right individually, and they will naturally set themselves right collectively. Thus the Bible deals only with the relationship between the individual and universal mind. Let the individual clearly understand the relation between these two, and all other relations will settle themselves on lines which, however varied in form, will always be characterized by individual Liberty working to the expression of perfect social harmony.

## Chapter 10
## THE TEACHINGS OF JESUS

### A System of Universal Principles

In this chapter I shall endeavor to give a connected idea of the general scope and purpose of the Master's teachings, the point of which we in great measure miss by taking particular sayings separately, and so losing the force which pertains to them by reason of the place they hold in his system as a whole. For, be it remembered, Jesus was teaching a definite system --- not a creed, nor a ritual, nor a code of speculative ethics, but a system resulting from the threefold source; spiritual inspiration, intellectual reasoning, and experimental observation, which are the three modes in which the Universal Mind manifests itself as Conscious Reasoning Power or "the Word". And therefore this system combines the religious, philosophical, and scientific characters, because it is a statement of the action of universal principles at the level where they find expression through the human mind.

### Individual Liberty

The great point to be noted in the teaching of Jesus is his statement of the absolute liberty of the individual. That was the subject of his first discourse in the synagogue of Nazareth (Luke 4:16); he continued his teaching with the statement, "the truth shall make you free" [John 8:32]; and he finished it with the final declaration before Pilate that he had come into the world to the end that he should bear witness to the Truth (John 18:37). Thus to teach the knowledge of Liberating Truth was the beginning, the middle, and the end of the great work which the Master set before him.

The other point is that this freedom is represented simply as the result of coming *to know the Truth*. If words mean anything, this means that Liberty in truth exists at the present moment, and that what keeps us from enjoying it is simply our ignorance of the fact. In other words, the Master's teaching is that the essential and therefore ever-present Law of each individual human life is absolute Liberty; it is so in the very nature of Being, and it is only our ingrained belief to the contrary that keeps us in bondage to all sorts of limitation.

Of course, it is easy to explain away all that the Master said by interpreting it in the light of our past experiences; but these experiences themselves constitute the very bondage from which he came to deliver us, and therefore to do this is to destroy his whole work. We do not require his teaching to go back to the belittling and narrowing influence of past experiences; we do that naturally enough so long as we remain ignorant of any other possibilities. It is just this being tied up that we want to get loose from, and he came to tell us that, when we know the Truth, we shall find we are not tied up at all. If we hold fast to the initial teaching of Genesis, that the Divine Principle makes things by itself *becoming* them, then it follows that when it becomes the individual man, it cannot have any other than its own natural movement in him --- that is, a continual pushing forward into fuller and fuller expression of itself, which therefore becomes fuller and fuller life in the individual; and consequently, anything that tends to limit the full expression of the individual life must be abhorrent to the Universal Mind expressing itself in that individuality.

Then comes the question as to the way in which this truth is to be realized; and the practical way repeated many times by the Master is very simple. It is only that we are to take this truth for granted. That is all. We may be ready to exclaim that this is a large demand upon our faith; but after all, it is the only way in which we ever do anything. We take all the operations of the Life-Principle in our physical body for granted, and what is wanted is a similar confidence in the working of our spiritual faculties.

## Trust

We trust our bodily powers because we assume their action as the natural Law of our being; and in just the same way we can only use our interior powers by tacitly assuming them to be as natural to us as any others. We must bear in mind that from first to last the Master's teaching was never other than a *veiled* statement of Truth: he spoke "the word" to the people in parables, and "without a parable spoke he not unto them" (Matt. 13:34). It is indeed added "and when they were alone he expounded all things to his disciples"; but if we take the interpretation of the parable of the sower as a sample [Matt. 13:3-9], we can see how very far these expositions were from being a full and detailed explanation.

The thickest and outermost veil is removed, but we are still very far from plain speaking among "the full-grown" which St Paul tells us was equally distant from his own writing to the Corinthians. I say this on the best authority, that of the Master himself. We might have supposed that in that last discourse, which commences with the fourteenth chapter of St John's Gospel, he had withdrawn the final veil from his teaching; but no, we have his own words for it that even this is a veiled statement of the Truth. He tells his disciples that the time when he shall show them plainly of "the Father" is still in the future (John 16:25).

He left the final interpretation to be given by the only possible interpreter, the Spirit of Truth, as the real significance of his words should in time dawn upon each of his hearers with an inner meaning that would be none other than the revelation of The

Sacred Name. As this meaning dawns upon us, we find that Jesus no longer speaks to us in proverbs, but that his parables tell us plainly of "the Father", and our only wonder is that we did not discern his true meaning long ago.

He is telling us of great universal principles which are reproduced everywhere and in everything with special reference to their reproduction on the plane of Personality. He is not telling us of rules which God has laid down in one way and could, had He chosen, have laid down in another, but of universal Laws which are therefore inherent in the constitution of Man. Let us, then, examine some of his sayings in this light.

### Truth

The thread on which the pearls of the Master's teaching are strung together is, "that Perfect Liberty is the natural result of knowing the Truth." "When you find what the Truth really is, you will know that the statement, "you are perfectly free" is the center from which all His other statements radiate [John 8:32]. But the final discovery cannot be made for you; you must each make it for *yourself*. Therefore, "he that hath ears to hear, let him hear" [Luke 14:35].

This is nowhere brought out more clearly than in the parable of the Prodigal Son [Luke 15:11-32]. The fact of sonship had never altered for either of the two brothers, but in different ways they each missed the point of their position as sons. The one limited himself by separating off a particular share of the Father's goods for himself, which, just because of being a limited share, was speedily exhausted, leaving him in misery and want.

The other brother equally limited himself by supposing that he had no power to draw from his Father's stores, but must wait till he in some way acquired a specific permission to do so, not realizing his inherent right, as his Father's son, to take whatever he wanted.

The one son took up a false idea of independence, thinking it consisted in separating himself and to be entirely "on his own", while the other, in his recoil from this conception, went to the opposite extreme and believed himself to have no independence at all.

The younger son's return, so far from extinguishing the instinct for Liberty, gratified it to the full by placing him in a position of honor and command in his Father's house; and the elder son is rebuked with the simple words, "Why wait for me to give you what is yours already? All that I have is thine". *It would be impossible to state the relation between the Individual Mind and the Universal Mind more clearly than in this parable,* or the two classes of error which prevent us from understanding and utilizing this relation.

## From Limitation to Infinity

The younger brother represents the man who, not realizing his own spiritual nature, lives on the resources of the lower personality until their failure to meet his needs drives him to look for something which cannot thus be exhausted, and eventually he finds it in the recognition of his own spiritual being as his inalienable birthright because he was made in the image and likeness of God and could not by any possibility have been created otherwise.

Gradually, as he becomes more and more conscious of the full effects of this recognition, he finds that "the Father" advances to meet him, until at last they are folded in each other's arms, and he realizes the true meaning of the words, "I and my father are *ONE*". Then he learns that Liberty is in union and not in separation, and realizing his identity with the Infinite, he finds that all its inexhaustible stores are open to him.

This is but simple fact, which becomes clear if we see that the only possible action of the undifferentiated Life-Principle must be to always press forward into fuller and fuller expression of itself, in particular forms of life, *in strict accordance with the conditions which each form provides for its manifestation.* And when anyone thoroughly grasps this principle of the differentiation, through form, of an entirely undistributed universal potential, then he will see that the mode of differentiation depends on the direction in which the specializing entity is reaching out and that there is no limit either of extent or of kind to the purposes for which he may employ the universal potential. But he can only do this by abiding in "the Father's" house, and by conforming to the rule of the house, which is the Law of Love.

### The Law of Universal Love

This is the only restriction, if it can be called a restriction, to avoid using our powers injuriously; and this restriction becomes self-obvious when we consider that the very thing which puts us in possession of this limitless power of drawing from the Infinite is the recognition of our identity with the Universal ***ONE***, and that any employment of our powers to the intentional injury of others is in itself a direct denial of that "unity of the Spirit which is the bond of peace".

The binding power of Universal Love is thus seen to be inherent in the very nature of the Liberty which we attain by the Knowledge of the Truth; but except this, there is no other restriction. Why? Because, by the very hypothesis of the case, we are employing First cause when we consciously use our creative power with the knowledge that our Thought is the individual action of the same Spirit which, in its Universal action, is both the Cause and the Being of every mode of manifestation; for the great fact which distinguishes First Cause from secondary causation is its entire independence of all conditions, because it is not the outcome of conditions but itself creates them --- it produces its own conditions step by step as it goes along. [For fuller explanation regarding the use of First Cause, see the first chapter of *"The Essential Thomas Troward"*.]

If, therefore, the Law of Love be taken as the foundation, any line of action can be worked out successfully and profitably; but this does not alter the fact that a higher degree of intelligence will see a much wider field of action than a lower one, and therefore if our field of activity is to grow, it can only be as a result of the growth of our intelligence; and consequently, the first use we should make of our power of drawing from the Infinite should be for steady growth in understanding.

## Companionship

Life is the capacity for action and enjoyment, and therefore any extension of the field for the exercise of our capacities is an increase of our own livingness and enjoyment; and so the continual companionship of the Spirit of Truth, leading us into continually expanding perception of the limitless possibilities that are open to ourselves and to the whole race, is the supreme Vitalizing Influence; and thus we find that the Spirit of Truth is identical with the Spirit of Life. *It is this consciousness of companionship that is the Presence of the Father*; and it is in returning to this Presence and dwelling in it that we get back to the Source of our own spiritual nature and so find ourselves in possession of boundless possibilities without any fear of misusing them, because we do not seek to be possessors of the Divine Power without being possessors of the Divine Love and Wisdom also.

And the elder brother represents the man who has not thrown off the Divine guidance as the younger brother had done, but who has realized it only in the light of a restriction. Always his question is, "Within what limits may I act?" and consequently, starting with the idea of limitation, he finds limitation everywhere; and thus, though he does not go into a far country like his brother, he relegates himself to a position no better than that of a servant, which he imagines himself to be by Divine appointment, not realizing he has imported them himself. But him also "the Father" meets with the gracious words, "Son, thou art ever with me, and all that I have is thine"; and therefore as soon as this elder brother becomes sufficiently enlightened to perceive that all the elements of restriction in his beliefs, save only the Law of Love, have no place in the ultimate reality of *Life*, he too re-enters the house, now no longer as a servant but as a son, and joins in the festival of everlasting joy.

We find the same lesson in the parable of the Talents [Matt. 25:14-30]. The use of the powers and opportunities we have, just where we are now, naturally opens up sequences by which still further opportunities, and consequently higher development of our powers, become possible; and these higher developments in their turn open the way to yet further expansion, so that there is no limit to the process of growth other than what we set it to be by denying or doubting the principle of growth in ourselves, which is what is meant by the servant burying his talent in the earth.

"The lord" is the Living Principle of Evolution which is generally recognized equally on all planes, and nothing has been more fully established by science than the Law that as soon as progress stops, retrogression begins.

But on the other hand, the employment of our faculties and opportunities, so far as we realize them, is, by the same Law, certain to produce its own reward. By being faithful over a few things, we shall become rulers over many things, for God is not unmindful to forget your labor of love, and so day by day we shall enter more and more fully into the joy of our Lord.

The same idea is repeated in the parable of the man who contrived to get into the wedding feast without the wedding garment [Matt. 22:2-14]. The Divine Marriage is the attainment by the individual mind of conscious union with the Universal Mind or "the Spirit"; and the feast, as in the parable of the Prodigal Son, signifies the joy which results from the attainment of Perfect Liberty, which means power over all the resources of the Universe, whether within us or around us.

Now, as I have already pointed out, the only way in which this power can be used safely and profitably is through that recognition of its Source which makes it in all points subservient to the Law of Love, and this was precisely what the intruder did not realize. He is the type of the man who fails in exactly the opposite way to the servant who buries his Lord's talent in the earth. This man has cultivated his powers to the uttermost, and so is able to enter along with the other guests. He has attained that Knowledge of the Laws of the spiritual side of Nature which gives him a place at the Table of the Lord which is the storehouse of the Infinite; but he has missed the essential point of all his Knowledge, the recognition that the Law of Power is one with the Law of Love, and so, desiring to separate the Divine Power from the Divine Love, and to grasp the one while rejecting the other, he finds that the very Laws of which he has used to try and make himself master overwhelm him with their own tremendousness and bind him hand and foot. The Divine Power can never be separated with impunity from the Divine Love and Guidance.

## Subjectivity

The parable of the unjust steward [Luke 16:1-13] is based upon the Law of the subjective nature of individual life. As in all the parables, "the lord" is the supreme Self-evolving Principle of the Universe which, relatively to us, is purely subjective because it acts in and through ourselves. As such, it follows the invariable Law of subjective mind, which is that of response to any suggestion that is impressed upon it with sufficient power. [I have discussed this subject at greater length in Chapter 12 of "The Essential Thomas Troward.]

Consequently, "the lord" does not dispute the correctness of the accounts rendered by the steward but, on the contrary, commends him for his wisdom in recognizing the true principle by which to escape the results of his past maladministration of the estate.

St Paul tells us that he is truly approved "whom the Lord commendeth", and the commendation of the steward is unequivocally stated by Jesus; and therefore we must realize that we have here the statement of some principle which harmonizes with the Life-giving tendency of the Universal Spirit. And this principle is the acceptance by "the Lord" of less than the full debt due to Him.

It is the statement of Ezekiel 18:21-22 that if the wicked man forsake his way, "he shall surely live and not die. All his transgressions that he hath committed shall not be mentioned unto him; in his righteousness that he hath done he shall live". It is what the Master speaks of as agreeing with the adversary while we are still in the way with him; in other words, it is the recognition that because the Laws of the Universe are not vindictive but simply causal, therefore the reversal of our former misemployment of First Cause, which in our case is our Thought demonstrated in a particular line of action, must necessarily result in the reversal of all those evil consequences which would otherwise have flowed from our previous wrong-doing.

## The Law of Suggestion

If we once realize the great truth stated in Psalm 18:26 and 2 Samuel 22:27, that the Divine Universal Spirit always becomes to us exactly the correlative of our own principle of action, and that it does so naturally by the Law of Subjective Mind, then it must become clear that it can have no vindictive power in it or, as the Bible expresses it, "Fury is not in Me" (Isaiah 27:4).

But for the very same reason, we cannot trifle with the Great Mind by trying to impress one character upon it by our thought while we are impressing another upon it by our actions. This is to show our ignorance of the nature of the Law with which we are dealing; for a little consideration will show us that we cannot impress two opposite suggestions at the same time. The man who tried to do so is described in the parable of the servant who threw his fellow-servant into prison after his own debt had been cancelled [Matt. 18:23-35]. The previous pardon availed him nothing, and he was cast into prison till he should pay the uttermost farthing.

The meaning becomes evident when we see that what we are dealing with is the supreme Law of our own being. We do not really believe what we do not act up to; if, therefore, we cast our fellow-servant into prison, no amount of philosophical speculation in an opposite direction will set us at liberty. Why? Because our action demonstrates that our real belief is in limitation. Such compulsion can only proceed from the idea that we shall be the poorer if we do not screw the money out of our fellow-servant, and this is to deny our own power of drawing from the Infinite in the most emphatic manner, and so to destroy the whole edifice of Liberty.

We cannot impress upon ourselves too strongly the impossibility of living by two contradictory principles at the same time. And the same argument holds good when we conceive that the debt is due to our injured feelings, our pride, and the like --- the principle is always the same; it is that the perfect Liberty of a true relationship between universal and individual mind places us above the reach of all such considerations such as criticism or put downs or slander, because, by the very hypothesis of being absolute freedom, it can create far more rapidly than any of our fellow-servants can run up debts; and our attitude towards those who are thus running up scores should be to endeavor to lead them into that region of fullness where the relation of debtor and creditor cannot exist because it becomes merged in the radiance of creative power.

## The Last Supper

Perhaps the most impressive of all Jesus' parables is that in which, on the night when He was betrayed, the Master expressed the great mystery of God and Man by symbolic action rather than by words. Here, at the last supper, we meet with a symbolical fact of the highest importance. The dramatization of the final truth of spiritual knowledge took place here.

Now as we all know, the supper was itself of supreme symbolical significance. It was the Jewish Passover and tradition tells us it was also the symbolic act by which, throughout antiquity, the highest initiates signified their identical realization of Truth, however apparently separated by outward forms or nationality.

We find these mystical emblems of bread and wine presented to Abraham by Melchizedek, himself the type of the man who had realized the supreme truth of the birth which is "without father, without mother, without beginning of days or end of years" (Hebrews 7:3); and therefore if we would grasp the full meaning of the Master's action on that last night, we must understand the meaning of the symbolic meal of which he and his followers had just partaken. Briefly stated, it is the recognition by the participant of his unity with, and power of appropriating, the Divine in its twofold mode of Spirit and Substance.

Science and Religion are not two separate things. They both have the same object: to bring us nearer and nearer to the point where we shall find ourselves in touch with the ***ONE*** Universal Cause. Therefore the two were never dissociated by the greatest thinkers of ancient times, and the inseparableness of energy and matter, which is now recognized by the most advanced science as the starting-point of all its speculations, is none other than the old, old doctrine of the identity of Spirit and ultimate Substance.

Now it is this twofold nature of the Universal First cause that is symbolized by the bread and wine. The fluid and the solid, or Spirit and Substance, as the two Universal supports of all manifested Forms --- these are the Universal principles which the two typical elements signify. But in order that the individual may be consciously benefited by them, he must recognize his own participation in them, and he denotes his Knowledge on this point by eating the bread and drinking the wine; and his intention in doing so is to signify his recognition of two great facts: one, that he lives by continually drawing from the Infinite Spirit in its twofold unity; and the other, that he not only does this automatically but also has the power to consciously differentiate the Universal Energy for any purpose that he will.

Now this combination of dependence and control could not be more perfectly symbolized than by the acts of eating and drinking. We cannot do without food, but it is at our own discretion to select what and when we shall eat. And if we realize the true meaning of "the Christ", we shall see that it is that principle of Perfected Humanity which is the highest expression of the Universal Spirit-Substance; and taken in this sense, the bread and wine are fitting emblems of the flesh and blood, or Substance and Spirit, of the "Son of Man", the ideal Type of all Humanity.

And so it is that we cannot realize the Eternal Life except by consciously partaking of the innermost Life-Principle, with due recognition of its true nature --- not meaning the mere observance of a ceremonial rite, however grand in its associations and however useful as a powerful suggestion; but meaning personal recognition of the Supreme Truth which that rite signifies.

This, then, was the meaning of the symbolic meal. It indicated the participant's recognition of his union with the Universal Spirit as being the supreme fact on which his individual life was based, the ultimate of all Truth.

## Voluntary Differentiation

And the Last Supper had yet another symbolic meaning.

The following message was graphically set forth and expanded upon as the Master's ministry in his mortal body was about to be terminated.

As ever, his theme was the perfect Liberty of the individual resulting from recognition of his true relation to the Universal Mind. The **ONE** great **I AM** is the Vine, the lesser ones are the branches. We cannot bear fruit except we abide in the Vine; but abiding in it there is no limit to the developments we may attain.

The Spirit of Truth will guide us into all Truth, and the possession of all Truth must carry the possession of all Power along with it; and since the Spirit of Truth can be none other than the Spirit of Life, to be guided into all Truth must be to be guided into the Power of an endless life.

This does not need our removal from the world: "I pray *NOT* that Thou shouldest take them out of the world, but that Thou shouldest keep them from evil" (John 17:15). What is needed is ceasing to eat of that poisonous fruit the tasting of which expelled Man from the Garden of Eden that he was designed to inhabit. The true recognition of the ***ONE*** leaves no place for any other; and if we follow the Master's direction not to estimate things by their superficial appearance, but by their central principle of being, then we shall find that nothing is evil in essence, and that the origin of evil is always a wrong application of what is good in itself, thus bringing us back to the declaration of the first chapter of Genesis, that God saw all that He had created, "and behold it was very good".

If, then, we realize that our Liberty resides in the creative power of our Thought, we shall see the immense importance of recognizing the essence of things as distinguished from the misplaced order in which we often first become acquainted with them. If we let our Thought dwell on an inverted order, we perpetuate that order; but if, going below the surface, we fix our Thought upon the essential nature of things and see that it is logically impossible for anything to be essentially bad which is a specific expression of the Universal Good, then we shall in our Thought call all things good, and so help to bring about that golden age when the old inverted order shall have passed away, and a new world of joy and liberty shall take its place.

This, then, is briefly the line followed by the Master's teaching, and his miracles were simply the natural outcome of his perfect recognition of his own principles. Already the unfolding recognition of these principles is beginning to produce the same results at the present day, and the number of well-authenticated cures effected by mental means increases every year. And this is precisely in accordance with Jesus' own prediction. He enumerated the signs which should follow those who really believed what he really taught, and in so saying he was simply making a statement of cause and effect. He never set up his power as proof of a nature different from our own; on the contrary, he said that those who learned what he taught should eventually be able to do still greater miracles, and he summed up the whole position in the words "the disciple when he is perfected shall be as his Master" (Luke 6:40).

## The Type of Perfected Humanity

When we realize what is accomplished in "the perfected man Christ Jesus", we see what is potential in ourselves; and since we have now reached the point beyond which any further evolution can only result from our conscious co-operation with the evolutionary principle, all our future progress depends on the extent to which we do recognize the potentialities contained in our own individuality.

Therefore to realize the manifestation of the Divine Ideal which Jesus demonstrated, and to love it, is the indispensable condition for attaining that access to "the Father" which means the full development in ourselves of all the powers of the Spirit.

By accepting this Divine Ideal as our own, we provide *the means by which* the Undifferentiated Universal Subconscious Mind becomes able to differentiate Itself into the particular and concrete expression of that Potential of Personality which is eternally inherent in It; and ***thus in each one who realizes the Truth which the Master taught, the Universal Mind attains an individualization capable of consciously recognizing Itself.*** To attain this is the great end of Evolution, and in thus gaining Its end the ***ONE*** becomes the ***MANY***, and the ***MANY*** return into the ***ONE*** --- not by an absorption depriving them of individual identity, which would be to stultify the entire operation of Evolution by simply ending it where it had begun, but by impressing upon innumerable individualities the perfect and completed likeness of that Original in the potential image of which they were first created.

The entire Bible is the unfolding of its initial statement that Man is made in the image of God, and the teaching of Jesus is the proclamation and demonstration of this Truth in its complete development, the Individual rejoicing in perfect Life and Liberty because of his conscious ***ONE***-ness with the Universal.

-----

## Summing it up

If this book has help the reader to see the intelligible sequence between cause and effect in God's creation of man its purpose has been fulfilled.

.

### *TRUTH CENTER Publishing*

-----

You can purchase Mr. Lode's books at:

Barnes and Noble - - - BN.com

Amazon.com

**truthcenter.blog.com**
his website

**Books are also available on Kindle**

--------------------

"Experiencing" THE HIDDEN MAGIC "at the Center"

**NEW AGE BIBLE**
"New Thought for the 3$^{rd}$ Millennium"

**A SHORT COURSE in Miracles**
"The Holy Bible's 3$^{rd}$ Testament"

**Finding the Essential "CHRIST"**
***"The Bible's last Testament"***

**A SEARCH FOR "SELF"**
"Experiencing A Course in Miracles"

**WINNING** "at the Game of Life"

**THE HIDDEN MAGIC** "at the Center"

The **GOSPEL of THOMAS** "In Modern Day Language"

The Essential **THOMAS TROWARD**

**THOMAS TROWARD'S**
Bible Mystery and Bible Meaning
"without the jargon"

Made in the USA
San Bernardino, CA
26 July 2014